HEROES FOR AN AGE OF ANXIETY

Standing on The Shoulders of Giants

Dana Huntley

CENTRAL PARK SOUTH PUBLISHING

Published by Central Park South Publishing 2024
www.centralparksouthpublishing.com

Typesetting and e-book formatting services by Victor Marcos

Contents

Archetypal Heroes

Faith Heroes

All-American Heroes

Heroes All Around Us

INTRODUCTION

Leaving Footprints on
the Sands of Time

There is no such thing as a "new normal." It may be many years before the full economic and social impact of our Covid-19 pandemic can be thoroughly weighed. By that time, of course, other world events, be they political, technological or pathological will have skewed human history and grabbed our attention.

What the months of raging epidemic gave us, however, was a pantheon of heroes. Health care professionals, long term care workers and first responders of every description unquestionably and knowingly put themselves in harm's way to minister to those infected and afflicted by the deadly coronavirus. Hundreds of them paid the ultimate sacrifice and left behind families and contributing lives.

Not that they labored in obscurity. We recognized their self-sacrifice and tireless devotion and lauded them as the heroes they were and are. Drive-bys, organized cheers, countless homemade signs and untold gestures of support from foodstuffs to fundraisers greeted and applauded the doctors, nurses, paramedics and care workers, as well as public service workers and grocery store employees who carried on while the rest of society was hunkered down. These were the heart-warming accounts covered by the media that were the bright spots through months of dark, depressing news coverage. Most of these heroes' individual stories will never be known.

Throughout history, both ancient and modern, natural disasters, wars, disease and political upheaval have yielded heroes—models that in one way or another we can emulate and whose example holds up for us the finest of human instincts.

At the very least, the coronavirus has given us a new appreciation for the social and personal anxiety people have lived with throughout so much of history—with plague, cholera, smallpox and war for a start. Perhaps it might also give us pause to look at what our society has valued as heroes, or more significantly what it has overlooked, discarded or forgotten. Let us think again about what is really important.

As an American society, we have taken our security for granted as well as the shallowness of our preoccupations. Celebrity belongs to the Kardashians, the want-to-be music idols, the rich bad boys of Hollywood and professional athletes we pay millions to entertain us. Coronavirus has unmasked us. While the world redefines our "new normal," let us set before us the thousand faces and forms of true heroism.

The Touchstones of Our Life

Among the most famous opening lines of literature is the first sentence spoken by the eponymous hero of Charles

Dickens' *David Copperfield*: "Whether I shall turn out to be the hero of my own life, or whether that role shall be reserved for someone else, these pages must show." At the very least, we would all like to turn out to be the heroes of our own lives. It would be a shame indeed, however, if we were the *only* heroes in our lives.

We need lots of heroes. The more men and women from history and today that we can mark as heroes and look up to and admire, the better. Heroes have shaped our world, and the heroes we have define and shape who we are both as a people and as individuals.

The late Victorian poet, critic and educator Matthew Arnold believed that history was determined by "touchstones," great individuals whose accomplishments by force of character and capability advanced society and civilization. Certainly, Arnold was correct at least in part. Whether we call them touchstones or heroes, from the days of the Pharaohs to yesterday's newspaper there is a phalanx of men and women across the centuries whose individual acts and lives have changed the course of history.

It is also true that heroes change us as indiviuals, in small ways and in everyday life. From our earliest days in this world, we have heroes: first Mom and Dad (if we are blessed), then siblings, grandparents, an aunt, a caregiver or family friend. As we become more aware of the outside world, our universe of heroes broadens: television heroes, like Sesame Street characters or worse, neighborhood figures and the first public figures of whom we're made aware, then teachers and peers. Our world is populated by people to whom we naturally look up and seek to emulate in some way. Throughout our school years and to the threshold of adulthood we mark our lives by changing touchstones—heroes who influence our choices and model the characteristics and values that become a part of us.

The motto of my high school academy was *Qui Esse Sumus Nunc Venimus*, which was rather presumptuous of a school that never taught Latin, but translates, "What we are to be, we are now becoming." It is true. What is set in front of us or what we set in front of ourselves influences us and contributes to what we will be a year or a generation from now. Until we have left home or graduated from college, what is set in front of us is largely determined by other people; when we are truly "on our own" or out in the "real" world, we choose for ourselves. The movies we see, books we read, music we select to hear, video games we play and television we watch: all contribute to molding a character that changes incrementally as long as we live. This is the *real* lifelong education for which our colleges tried to prepare us. Just so, everyone writes their own book of heroes every day, and it *is* their own book—a story of their life.

Heroism is a Personal Thing

After all, there can be no such thing as an *objective* book of heroes. Heroism lies in the eye of the beholder, as we shall see. We cannot see or perceive or acknowledge heroism that might exist apart from ourselves and the way we view and value the world. I could not write a book of heroes who were not my own. The heroes profiled in any list inevitably reflect whoever it is who happens to be choosing them.

Every book of narrative non-fiction reflects the world view of its writer. I hate it when I have to read halfway through a text to find out where an author has hid her or his sympathies. With such a topic as this in particular, however, it is only fair play to nail my piratical colors to the mast at the start of the sail.

My own list of heroes is long indeed, and not yet completed, but the stories of heroism told here still come from my own upbringing, identity and reading. I am a broad-church Christian and a classical humanist. My instincts are intrinsically libertarian, believing in the moral primacy of the individual, not the State. I believe in the inherited culture of Western Civilization. I come off a dairy farm in New Hampshire from families that were Yankee yeomen of colonial Puritan stock. I am afraid that is not a very fashionable or politically correct background these days. It is a classically American background, though, and that is reflected in the heroes that bubbled forth in this story.

But We're All in this Together

Two people whom I much admire, though we are quite unlike in many ways, are Denzel Washington and the late Joe Lieberman. Their backgrounds, interests, priorities, education and values are their own, and our three lists of heroes would be quite different. At the same time, compared to the lists that might be generated by Jaques Chirac, Ozzy Osbourne, Imelda Marcos or Osama bin Laden, Denzel, Joe and I would find quite a lot of common ground. There is a commonality of experience and identity in being an American (or being an Australian or Austrian) that results in shared values and a shared way of looking at the world. In particular, there is an American way of looking at people and their worth as individuals, a respect for personhood and for the dignity of human life.

At the same time, American culture and society are derivative from our historic roots in Great Britain. With American hegemony of a continent bridging the Atlantic and Pacific, we are often accused of being insular and isolated from the rest of the world. In fact, it is our historical and cultural ties to Britain (and our shared ethos with the other "settler colonies" of Canada, Australia, New Zealand and what Churchill calls "the English-speaking world"), that create our strongest connection to the much wider world beyond our shores. Many of our models of heroism, King Arthur and Henry V, the Duke of Wellington and William Wallace, come to us from Britain as part of that shared cultural ethos as well.

As the pace of Hispanic migration in particular, legal or otherwise, continues into the States and the tensions of our world culture-clash between the West and Islam continue, defining our American identity becomes no easier now than it was in the late 1700s. Still, that old school motto of mine applies as truly to nations and societies as it does to individuals: What we are to be, we are now becoming. Searching for heroes that reflect who we are and have been may help us remember what we want to be.

Early American poet Henry Wadsworth Longfellow is not read as much as he was a century ago. Like fashions in everything else, fashions in poetry change. In the first decades of our American republic, however, Longfellow captured at several points the unique and emerging American identity. Among those themes, Longfellow champions the American spirit that believes in action, in doing, in effort: that in America each individual has the capacity to be a hero, to leave footprints on the sands of time:

A Psalm of Life

Tell me not, in mournful numbers,
*   Life is but an empty dream! –*
For the soul is dead that slumbers,
*   And things are not what they seem.*

Life is real! Life is earnest!
*   And the grave is not its goal;*
Dust thou art, to dust returnest,
*   Was not spoken of the soul.*

Not enjoyment, and not sorrow,
*   Is our destined end or way;*
But to act, that each to-morrow
*   Find us farther than to-day.*

Art is long, and Time is fleeting,
*   And our hearts, though stout and brave,*
Still, like muffled drums, are beating
*   Funeral marches to the grave.*

In the world's broad field of battle,
*   In the bivouac of Life,*
Be not like dumb, driven cattle!
*   Be a hero in the strife!*

Trust no Future, howe'er pleasant!
*   Let the dead Past bury its dead!*
Act,-act in the living Present!
*   Heart within, and God o'erhead!*

Lives of great men all remind us
We can make our lives sublime,
And, departing, leave behind us
Footprints on the sands of time;

Footprints, that perhaps another,
Sailing o'er life's solemn main,
A forlorn and shipwrecked brother,
Seeing, shall take heart again.

Let us, then, be up and doing,
With a heart for any fate;
Still achieving, still pursuing,
Learn to labor and to wait.

The heroes profiled here have all left footprints on the sands of time. Some of them are household names and some are not. As their collective story unfolded, they grouped themselves into four broad families. First, there are the Classical Heroes. These are the men and women for whom the term "hero" was originally invented. Next, there are Archetypal Heroes. These are individuals whom by their lives and actions model heroism for us in all its different manifestations. No, I am sure this is not a comprehensive or excluding list.

Faith Heroes is a third category. Whether one is a person of Christian faith or not, there is no doubt that throughout history faith has been one of the most significant motivators of heroic life and action. Finally, there are the All-American Heroes. These are heroes who, while their lives would be no less heroic lived elsewhere, illustrate, illuminate, and define our own uniquely

American society and its history. Though there are a few obvious inclusions here, there are more obvious exclusions.

How I have described these men and women, however, is not categorically exclusive by any means. Jeanne Mance, motivated to a life of healing by her love for God, is a faith hero. Obviously, Ronald Reagan and Helen Keller are American heroes. And all our American heroes are archetypes of one heroic fashion or another. In fact, all of the heroes here can be described in many ways.

In sum, these pages proffer an inspiring romp through the centuries, meeting great men and women of all walks of life who may still have something to teach us today about life and about what we want our tomorrow to be.

CHAPTER 1

The Hero Through History

O, To Be a Hero!

In the climactic scene of *An Officer and a Gentleman*, a determined Richard Gere, resplendent in the dress whites of a Naval officer, strides onto the factory floor and sweeps Debra Winger into his arms carrying her away from the dinginess of her life into happily-ever-after. In the background, gravelly Joe Crocker sings: "Love lift us up where we belong, where the eagles fly on the mountain high. Love lift us up where we belong . . . ." There are few of us who do not in one fashion or another long for that personification of something to sweep us from the here-and-now of our daily existence into the uplands where we know that we belong. There are few of us who do not long for heroes. And most of us hope that if our moment arrived upon the stage, we in turn would acquit ourselves as heroes.

In the beginning, the hero was the potent and god-like warrior. Accompanied by courage, great skill and strength, the hero put himself in harm's way and emerged victorious and triumphant. It was in combat that he proved himself—and lifted up before all the virtues to which all men aspired. Song and story carried the deeds of the hero beyond him and before him.

In classical days, the great epic poetry of the Greeks and Romans celebrated the gods and the god-qualities in heroes. Odysseus and Aeneas, Hercules and Jason: sometimes the line between god and mortal itself seemed blurred in the telling of mighty deeds. In fact, the venerable Oxford English Dictionary defines "hero" first in these classical origins: "A man of superhuman strength, courage or ability, favored by the gods; a demigod."

In the tumultuous Dark Ages after Rome's fall, heroes became more localized—often those defending the regional populace against the aggression of outsiders, maybe a Celtic chieftain repelling the incursions of the Anglo-Saxons, or in turn an Anglo-Saxon thane repelling the incursions of the Vikings. Through the Middle Ages, Crusaders found inspiration in the warrior-heroes of classical literature and in the Old Testament warrior-heroes of the Bible, and they set off to the Holy Land to become heroes themselves.

Yes, the hero was still a warrior, because the world was war-like and unstable. Like a kid growing up in Minneapolis whose father owned an auto body shop might grow up expecting to go into and inherit the family business, almost any male child growing up in the medieval world knew the possibility that sooner or later they would find themselves in mortal combat. Life was nasty, brutish and short—as the saying goes. How one would acquit one's self in battle was a front-burner preoccupation of adolescence and manhood. Let's face it; the prospect of being hacked to death by a dull blade wielded in battle fury isn't an appealing one. What other qualities any given hero might possess, they have had to overcome their fear.

It was physical courage that was required in that world, and an attribute of character far more visible and important in daily life throughout the Middle Ages than in our own time. Thus, the second definition of "hero" in the OED: "A man, now also a woman, distinguished by the performance of extraordinarily brave or noble deeds; an illustrious warrior." The hero is now a man or woman, at least, not someone godlike and removed from ordinary human experience.

During Trafalgar Week, celebrating the 200th anniversary of Lord Nelson's fatal victory over the combined French and Spanish Fleet, I was the guest on BBC Radio Five *Up All Night*—a call-in talk show. The subject that evening was British heroes. Lord Nelson, all agreed, was a good representative of the national British hero.

That Battle of Trafalgar Lord Nelson won wasn't his first. The swashbuckling seaman had already proved himself in the Battle of Copenhagen, the Battle of the Nile and sundry other sea action. In the process, he lost an eye and an arm, but that was little enough price to pay for the glory he consciously sought. Then, at Trafalgar, Nelson's risky and unorthodox plan of battle completely destroyed French and Spanish power upon the seas—the action left Britannia ruling the waves for a century and smoothed the way for the Pax Britannia. Standing on the deck of his flagship *HMS Victory*, the pint-sized admiral was struck in the shoulder by a round fired by a French sniper on the yardarm of a nearby ship. Lying on the orlop deck, Nelson heard of his great victory before he expired of his wounds.

When they finally transported Lord Nelson's corpse back to London, pickled in brandy, the admiral was given a public demonstration and state funeral of outlandish proportions. If the cocky, self-promoting, licentious sailor may have lacked universal admiration in life, in death Lord Nelson was the epitome of a warrior hero. To this day, nearly every market town and city of significance in Britain has a statue or monument of some kind to Lord Nelson. Punctuating the point, of course, is the mammoth Nelson monument that dominates Trafalgar Square—in the absolute heart of London. It's a stroke of pure English irony that the huge bronze lions that surround and guard the base of Nelson's Monument were cast from the cannons of ships he defeated. Nelson would be so pleased; he *wanted* to be a hero.

The hero didn't remain just the warrior, however. As Western Civilization marched on, our concept of the hero has broadened considerably. By Nelson's day and into our own, we have come recognize that heroism can be embodied by nobility in other attributes of character and endeavor.

Beyond recognizing figures like Lord Nelson, Winston Churchill and the Duke of Wellington as national heroes, listeners who joined the BBC on-air dialog with me shared far more localized and personal ideas of personified heroism. Among the heroes mentioned by listeners were legendary Yorkshire cricketer Geoffrey Boycott, World War I nurse Edith Cavell and a lifeboat crew off the Norfolk coast who gave their lives saving others in the North Sea.

As BBC listeners suggested, there are other kinds of hero besides warriors and other kinds of heroism besides valor in battle. Florence Nightingale, for instance. had the moxie to go to the Crimea when disease made corpses of more British soldiers than did bullets. Nightingale made the connection between sanitation and health, and more than any single individual created the profession of modern nursing. Little wonder she went on to become a legend in her own time.

Rosa Parks took a calculated risk, and took a seat and wouldn't get up, and wouldn't give up, and with great dignity became a hero. Alan Shepherd strapped himself in to a little, bitty capsule and became the first American hurled into the unknown of space travel, and became a hero. We justly applaud and make objects of admiration of those who risk, struggle and accomplish in almost any serious arena of human endeavor.

The third definition of "hero" recorded in the OED explains: "A man, now also a woman, admired and venerated for his or her achievements and noble qualities in any field." Where the heroic virtues are displayed, there is a hero.

The Hero in the Marketplace

We have always needed heroes. From the earliest days of civil society, mankind seems to have had an innate desire to seek, elevate and celebrate heroes. Who is regarded the hero, what is regarded as heroic, however, as we see, changes considerably with time and place. It varies as do individuals and societies. The hero is a reflection of our greater self. And our self, of course, is a product of our times, our place and our society. The hero personifies that which we aspire to be—that which we hope we should prove to be if Fate put us in the circumstances that makes heroes. Whether or not there is the capacity for heroism in each of us, who knows? Many folk will live their entire lives without being tested. Or testing themselves.

But yes, everyone should have heroes, the more the better. We need heroes. Having people to admire and esteem is good for us, and not just as children growing up. Aspiration is the ultimately human characteristic. It is certainly *one* thing that separates us from the animals. Without aspiration there is no hope that as individuals and as a society we can be better than we are.

We need heroes because of their example. Mother Theresa, Marie Curie and Jesse Owens, Eli Weisel and Martin Luther. Heroes give us those touchstones by which we can define our lives and take the measure of ourselves. Being conscious of who our heroes are is like weighing ourselves; it gives us a measure of our changing character.

Are Heroes Still Around?

> *"The Hero can be Poet, Prophet, King, Priest or what you will, according to the kind of world he finds himself born into."*
>
> *Thomas Carlyle*

For the past hundred years or so our Western culture has floated about the idea that heroes are gone, that we do not have them anymore. When World War I bankrupted Europe of its treasure chests and its young men, and doomed its colonial empires, it seemed that civilization itself was in terminal decline and the age of the hero passed.

T.S. Eliot became a voice describing this void of heroes, in his famous poems "The Wasteland" and "The Lovesong of J. Alfred Prufrock." As A.N. Wilson writes of "Prufrock" in *After the Victorians*: "For the sun is setting, as the women talk of Michelangelo, on European civilization. Philosophy can draw no conclusions, it can only stammer and hesitate. Nor is there room or a place any longer for heroism. Even that most dithering and uncertain of heroes, Hamlet, has not a place on this stage."

In its original sense, yes, the classic hero is harder to find and more difficult to emulate today. In the arena of war, battle itself has become depersonalized by mechanization. First, in the American Civil War, then with increasing ferocity in World War I, the killing of men became removed from hand to hand combat where strength, agility, skill with weaponry and personal courage determined the outcome—and where you felt the blood and the fear and saw the face of the man whom you engaged. The open field set-piece battles that were the stage for the warrior-hero of Greece and Rome and that characterized warfare into the late 19th century have been rendered obsolete by technology.

Though we recognize the courage and skill of our soldiers in Afghanistan, Iraq or the Persian Gulf, certainly in the last generation American society as a whole has lost its respect and veneration for the warrior class and its heroes. Very few little boys and girls these days want to grow up to be soldiers.

In the 1800s, Victorian England was on the rise as the dominant world power, and the sun never set on its Empire. Heroes were popular, and the heroic virtues cultivated. Thomas Carlyle was a perceptive essayist and commentator on his times. In *Heroes and Hero Worship*, Carlyle wrote, "No sadder proof can be given by a man of his own littleness than disbelief in great men." Old Carlyle, in fact, believed history's progress was the sum of accomplishments of Great Men. [We can read "Great Individuals" these days, of course.]

Society used to think it good to have heroes—to hold up people to emulate. The social consciousness assumed that we could be better than we are; that our humanity and our character were a work in progress. Now, we do not necessarily believe that as a culture any longer.

We have undergone a leveling in society now—no one can claim to be morally better than anyone else. No one is recognized to have or can claim with impunity a superior character (especially superior to our own). As W.S. Gilbert's character observes in *The Gondoliers*: "If every one is somebody, than no one's anybody." That's exactly what good portions of our society wants. A world where no one is anybody, and where everyone is special. Huh?

Perhaps in contemporary society it is more difficult for us to honor and recognize real heroes because we have democratized the word. Rather than regard as a hero the individual of extraordinary accomplishment and valor, we want the hero to be just like us—and someone *we* might be. Instead of the hero being found on the battlefield in service of a great cause, now we have the heroes at high school basketball games, recycling drives, video game tournaments and church fairs.

The inflation of meaning in the word "hero" is hardly a unique phenomenon in our language today. Accidents and events are called "tragic" in our lives that are at worst inconvenient. We have "gourmet" cooks who cannot make a white sauce without a recipe. There has been a general inflation in superlatives; objects and experiences are termed "great" that are at best fleetingly enjoyable.

Unprincipled and intrinsically cowardly individuals, of course, acknowledge no heroes. There have always been those who believed that you could strengthen the weak by weakening the strong. That you could raise yourself by lowering the esteem accorded others. It is true. We worship heroes only if we aspire to embody the heroic ourselves.

Still, it is a myth that in modern society we have no place for heroes. Despite all the cultural undercurrents, heroes *do* still exist, and they are important to our society, to our civilization and to us. What father does not want to be a hero to his children? Which of us do not consciously or unconsciously scan our world for those we can admire, emulate and find a source of personal inspiration?

It's an Angle of Vision

A Ford and a Toyota get into a mix-up at a busy midtown intersection. There are broken glass, crushed fenders and rising tempers. As the police arrive to do their pickup work, statements are taken from witnesses to the accident standing on different street corners. What these witnesses saw and how they describe it depends upon their angle of vision and their level of attention. Whose fault or innocence they see in events may well literally depend upon their point of view.

A hero in one heart, hamlet or country may just as easily be a villain elsewhere. Are William Wallace and

Owyn Glendwyr British heroes? Wallace has been a hero to generations of nationalistic Scots; to the English, he was a boil on the backside. So too, Owyn Glendwyr. The 15th-century self-proclaimed Welsh prince may have been a courageous hero to the Celtic Welsh, but he was a nuisance to England for a decade. Every war has two sides at least; the warrior hero cannot exist without an enemy—to whom he is no hero. Admiral Lord Nelson is no hero in France. William Tecumsah Sherman will never be a hero in Atlanta.

We might recognize heroic traits in individuals, but the traits themselves are not sufficient for our emotive selves to recognize the heroic. The characteristics or actions of heroism have to be embodied in a cause or action with which we sympathize. No matter how personally courageous or self-sacrificing the actions of a Nazi soldier during World War II may have been, to whom is that person a hero? *Is* that person a hero? Not to most of us.

Sometimes becoming a hero is an accident of time and place. From Puget Sound to Biscayne Bay and across the globe, there are men and women going about their daily lives with conviction and purpose who have no idea that life's circumstances will make heroes of them tomorrow or next month or when they are old and gray.

Winston Churchill became the hero by that combination of character and opportunity. He seemed to live confident that destiny would bring him where it did. Churchill was looking for that confluence of time and place where he could be a hero. More often, though, the moment and the destiny arrive for those who do not know that it is coming, and who have no dreams of heroism.

Awaking on September 11, 2001, hundreds of individuals who were to become heroes that day took their first cup of coffee unaware of what would unfold in their lives through the hours just ahead. Thousands of folks were making their way to a workday at the towers of the World Trade Center and at the Pentagon, and scores of passengers and crew had an early morning arrival at Boston's Logan Airport for rush hour flights. And thousands of NYPD officers and NYFD firefighters were taking their shifts across the city; medical personnel—EMTs, emergency room staff, ambulance drivers, doctors—and disaster response people at the Salvation Army and the Red Cross started another unpredictable day in the Big Apple.

Then, of course, all hell broke loose across the Northeast. Commandeered passenger planes struck one, then the other, of the looming New York City skyscrapers, and one after another, they fell. Two hundred miles to the south, in the airspace of the nation's capital, one struck straight into the side of the Pentagon. In a well-crafted act of guerilla warfare, undercover warriors of Islamic triumphalism struck a blow at icons of American business and government. Thousands of people died; thousands of families were shattered forever. And out in western Pennsylvania a determined group of passengers took Flight 93 into the ground and became heroes.

Heroes were born by the moment. As real and tragic as the loss of every individual who died in the attacks of that day remains, it was not often the victims themselves who were the heroes by being in that time and place. The heroes were the rescue personnel who thronged to the dust-choked rubble of lower Manhattan, who took great risk upon themselves to save life, recover bodies and dig the city through the ensuing days. And those in Washington and New York who put their lives on hold to tend to the countless victims of the attack—medically, spiritually, emotionally and materially.

The events of that September morning and its aftermath are indelibly etched in the minds of millions. It is of one those moments in history, like the bombing of Pearl Harbor and Kennedy's assassination, where everyone remembers the moment in their own lives.

The Hero is an Individual

Heroism is the trait of an individual; it is not a group characteristic. A person can make the heroic decisions for herself or himself, but no one can make those decisions for someone else. While another individual may inspire and successfully encourage the heroism of another individual, no one but the person can act or choose for themselves.

Certainly there can be concerted acts of heroism and heroic bravery, like the concerted action aboard American Flight #214 on 9/11, but the members of a heroic concerted action are each heroes in their own right as individuals.

Every society and culture values the qualities of self-sacrifice, tenacity, self-denial and courage that contribute to the hero. No society places such a high value upon the heroic and glorifies heroism, however, as does the Western civilization of America. Our world view draws upon the twin cultural pillars of the classical world (Hellenism) and the Biblical world (Hebraism), and mixes it with northern European Protestantism. As a culture, we place more value and responsibility on the individual than do many historic and present societies.

In fact, that emphasis upon individual value and achievement is part of what we call the Enlightenment.

The ideas of the Enlightenment floated around Europe through the late 17th and 18th centuries. The Enlightenment celebration of human reason, individual worth and a belief in natural law that was championed by people we have heard of like Voltaire, Immanuel Kant, John Locke, Jonathan Swift and Adam Smith was shared as well by fellows like Thomas Paine, Thomas Jefferson and Ben Franklin. While the Enlightenment movement of ideas fell across Europe, there it fell upon centuries-old societies and ways of life. Through the American Revolution and our defining charter documents, America became the first nation-state conceived by the principles of the Enlightenment. We were built for heroes!

Europe, on the other hand, has never forgiven us. More than other cultures, we see individual action rather than impersonal forces in the course of history. We have more famous women and men in our short history than do other cultures and we praise them more. We have always had a climate that makes them.

So, Who Is a Hero These Days?

Yes, so how do we define heroes and heroism early in the 21st century? Who are our heroes? Perhaps as good a question is: Who should they be? There are lots of ways to ask the question. At the King's Court Tavern, where I tossed this topic around with the regulars, Joey opines that a hero to him is someone for whom he would do anything that was asked of him, anything he could. Beth actually recalled Carl Sandburg and Edward R. Murrow sitting at the kitchen table when she was a girl; she picked Sandburg. The effervescent Sarah wants to see heroes in the common sphere of daily life; her heroes are all the unsung caregivers. Justin sees heroes in ecological engineers and biotechnicians. Most alarming, however, as I have queried folks for months about their heroes, is that so many people, particularly young people, do not have any. There are some half-hearted votes for Mother, understandably, but many people do not have any heroes they admire, look up to or seek to emulate.

We have an American culture that has been fragmenting since the 1960s and a Western Civilization that has been diluting its identity for a century, so it is really not surprising that in American and Western society today we undoubtedly have a far more diffuse idea of what constitutes a hero. Whatever benefits have been gained by our modern embrace of multiculturalism, they have come at the expense of our unity of common American identity. Two generations ago we would have had a much more unified vision of what constitutes the strong, the noble, the right—and the heroic.

Our society knows beyond doubt now that we live unaware amid heroes from every background and walk of life. Among the many aftereffects of the coronavirus pandemic, may we reap a renewed appreciation for the commonality of our American values and the shoulders of giants they stand on.

Hunting for Heroes

So, let's look for heroes. Let's look for those giants on whose shoulders we can stand.

There are so many different kinds of heroism, the personal attributes heroism requires are equally as varied. The test of moral courage displayed by a Dietrich Bonhoeffer, for instance, as he faced a Nazi execution requires something different than withstanding physical torture, for instance. The qualities of character are different still that motivated the accomplishments of Rosa Parks or Alan Shepherd.

One kind of heroism draws upon a combination of character and chance. Whatever heroic capacity an individual might have, it requires that they be in the right place and time, the right circumstances of life to draw upon and test and bring to the stage those qualities of heroism. It takes opportunity created by will or providence to forge heroism out the materials in the individual character.

Most of us, in fact, have the raw ingredients for both heroism and cowardice in us. Oh, we might well survive one variety of heroic challenge if it were placed in front of us, but in another arena of life we would shrink into the wallpaper. Yes, I might well risk my neck for cause or kin, but if you and I are in the wilderness and I have to perform an emergency appendectomy on you, don't expect a heroic outcome.

Another kind of heroism combines achievement and unspecified "noble qualities." Achievement by itself is not enough. The noble quality we most recognize is that heroes give of themselves for others. This is heroism born of serving. It is Father Flanagan devoting his life to Boys Town, Clara Barton giving birth to the Red Cross, Mother Theresa succoring the slums of Calcutta. It is characterized by commitment and caring for people.

Ability is a given. Whatever heroic action or life is celebrated, nothing would be celebrated unless the honored individual possessed the ability to accomplish their heroic achievement. We would not be celebrating either, unless the heroic individual had taken advantage of the ability they did have. Beyond sheer ability, however, those things we think of as heroic qualities are courage, success in the face of adversity, dedication, selflessness, faith, confidence, resolve and a clear sense of what is right.

What is sure is that throughout history heroism has existed in many different manifestations, motives and causes. From every walk and station of life men and women show us a heroic way.

CHAPTER 2

Odysseus: the Epic Hero

The whole idea of the hero comes from the Classical World—the historic foundations of what we consider Western Civilization. With some limited input from other ancient cultures, that means the Greek civilization of 6-4th centuries BC and the Roman republic and empire of 200BC-circa 400AD. Their histories and mythologies glorify and honor warriors like Hercules and Jason and the Argonauts. From their literature and legends does our concept of the heroic emerge.

In the beginning there was Odysseus. He was the original archetypal hero. Homer told the tale in his epic poem *The Odyssey*. It is very possible you were painfully introduced to the story by an enthusiastic high school English teacher.

Back a few thousand years BC there was the Trojan War. It was in all the papers. Odysseus was a captain and gallant warrior, a local king from the Greek island of Ithaca. At the war's conclusion, Odysseus and his men set sail from Troy (on the Turkish mainland) to return home. Along the way, they run into some challenges in the Mediterranean—assorted perils, monsters, battles and sundry adventures like the Sirens and Scylla and Carybdis. In each case, Odysseus manages to out-smart, out-fight, out-fox the natural or supernatural danger.

In the end, it takes Odysseus 10 years to get home to his wife Penelope and his island kingdom. In the meantime, presuming Odysseus to be dead, suitors have come to seek Penelope's widowed hand in marriage. Odysseus lands home and asserts his kingly and husbandly authority and, of course, has to kill them all. And Odysseus and Penelope, at least, live happily ever after.

Odysseus is the prototype of the classical hero. Born out of the ethos of the ancient Greek world, Odysseus has strength, courage, craft and cunning. There is a willingness for self-sacrifice and a selflessness about him, but there is as well a callous willingness to inflict pain and death. He was the perfect soldier in a society that ennobled warriors. Today, these are the same qualities of character and ability that distinguish the great soldier—superbly human in body and sensibility, yet able to distance himself from humanity's softer instincts to accomplish the soldier's job.

The Romans were impressed. The great Latin poet Virgil borrowed from Odysseus's tale in *The Aeneid*, with his hero Aeneas wandering after the Trojan wars and ending up contributing to the birth of Rome. In fact, we have been impressed ever since, and the story of Odysseus (often Latinized as Ulysses) has been retold and adapted ever since by the Western cultures. In Victorian times, Alfred, Lord Tennyson made him the eponymous hero of one of his most memorable poems. In Tennyson's "Ulysses," our hero is now an older king, settled years later back on Ithaca and still longing for adventure. He affirms the heroic impulse, even though the passing years have taken their toll on him and his men, they remain:

> *One equal temper of heroic hearts, made weak by*
> *time and fate,*
> *But strong in will: to strive, to seek, to find and*
> *not to yield."*

There's another element to *The Odyssey*, however, and to Odysseus. Our classical hero is not *simply* a warrior. He is also a quester. The journey from the battlefields of Troy that took Odysseus 10 years to accomplish was a quest. And while the clear object of that journey was home, there were things to be done along the way, deeds to accomplish, self-discoveries to be made, adventures to be experienced. And in all, the hero's qualities of mind, heart and body would be challenged. After all, if it was just as simple as sailing back from the coast of Turkey to the Greek Islands, even 3,000 years ago a few days would have done the job.

Questers are few in this world. Most people are content enough to go through life processing the life experience that comes their way without feeling any internal sense of urgency to actually make sense of it all. Some small percentage of folk, however, are hard-wired to want to know the questions and the answers, whose psyche echoes Ulysses:

> *Yet all experience is an arch wherethro'*
> *Gleams that untravell'd world whose margin fades*
> *For ever and for ever when I move.*

. . . .

And this gray spirit yearning in desire
To follow knowledge like a sinking star
Beyond the utmost bound of human thought.

Those who seek experiential knowledge and non-contingent truth seem to be harder and harder to find. Perhaps it is not true—but simply part of the jeremiad of every generation. Still, for the first time in human history the dominant world view of society predicates that there is no such thing as unconditional truth. If there is no truth to be found, that would certainly decrease the motivation for seeking it.

Our literature is full of questers who have followed in Odysseus's footsteps, from Sir Percival to Willie Loman, from Lemuel Gulliver to Frodo Baggins. In one form or another the quest is a part of the mythic ethos of every people. That story is told in Joseph Campbell's *The Hero with a Thousand Faces*, and it is a great one.

As a classical hero, Odysseus models two kinds of heroism. He is both the warrior hero and the questing hero. It is tough enough to emulate one. It is as true in our day as in the Greek world of the 5th century BC, however, that if you are going to undertake the quest, you had best be prepared to be a warrior.

Yes, every people in every time, every country and tribe, have their own heroes, and their own standards of heroism. In one fashion or another, however, the warrior and the quester are universal heroic models. If we find heroism an element lacking in our own society at the start of 21st century, it is perhaps because we value these qualities less than we used to.

We still recognize and fully appreciate individual acts of courage, bravery and self-sacrifice upon the battlefield; our soldiers in Iraq and Afghanistan have proved themselves every bit the equal to the legacy of valor upon the battlefield that American warriors have always earned. But the role of the warrior has faded from prominence since the Second World War. Both Korea and Vietnam saw plenty of individual heroes, but those conflicts did change our way of life. Three generations of Americans now have no memory of when warrior heroes were palpably felt necessary for our physical and emotional security. None of us hope we may be now paying a price for that dearly-won, inherited impulse to peace.

The Greeks and Romans, however, are not the only ancient sources for our notions of the hero.

CHAPTER 3

David: The Biblical Hero

So Samuel took the horn of oil and anointed him in
the presence of his brothers, and from that day on
the Spirit of the Lord came upon David in power.
                                        I Samuel 16:13

The Hellenistic world is only one of the ancient threads of our concept of heroism. The other is the Hebrew world of the Bible. Both the Old and New Testaments are full of heroes in many forms and guises. From Abraham to Paul the pages of scripture are filled with men and women whose qualities of courage are matched with qualities of faith. The Patriarchs, the prophets and judges of Israel, the followers of Jesus's ministry and the Apostles who carried the Gospel across the ancient world: every book of scripture defines or describes heroism in action.

The lesson of heroism they all provide, whether it be Moses, Joshua, Esther, Peter or Stephen, is that courage can be empowered by faith in God. Certainly, it was their example that inspired the martyrs of Christianity's first centuries and has continued to inspire men and women through the centuries to undertake deeds and lives of moral and physical heroism for the sake of their beliefs. While it is admittedly a weakness of Christians to want to define the *true* heroes of faith in their own image, the roster of Christians emboldened by biblical heroes is diverse indeed: Joan of Arc and Martin Luther King, Oliver Cromwell, Mother Theresa and David Livingstone, Augustine of Hippo, John Hus and Aimee Semple McPherson.

Trying to explain faith in God to someone who has never really known it is like trying to describe a sunset or a rainbow to someone who is color-blind. God gives the gift of faith, but it is a gift that everyone is invited to receive. 'Tis a conundrum indeed. Countless books have been written, sermons preached and discussions held to try to explain faith. Countless more will be. For our purposes, though, it is sufficient to remember Pascal's pithy summation, "The heart has its reasons that reason does not know." When faith motivates, it can motivate completely.

There isn't a kid who has ever gone to Sunday School who does not remember the story of David, called "the man after God's own heart." His life and leadership, failures and victories are recorded in the books of I and II Samuel. David was not yet a man, however, when he was faced with the defining moment of his life. He was still a youth, whose responsibility it was to tend his father's sheep out in the dry scrubland of Palestine.

David's older brothers were soldiers in the Israelite army of King Saul. They were arrayed against an army of the Philistines—a confederation of tribes that occupied southwestern Canaan who were known for their skill with ironwork. Skirmishes had long been fought between the Philistines and the Hebrews. Now, they set themselves against Israel with a champion warrior whose name was Goliath. With armies encamped against each other in uneasy anticipation of battle, for 40 days Goliath came out into no man's land and challenged the Hebrews to decide their war by sending against him a man to engage in single combat.

Goliath got no takers, and little wonder. To begin with, Goliath had something of a pituitary problem; I Samuel 17 records that his height was 9'4". Beyond that, he was wearing the most advanced body armor of his day. While I have no doubt there were plenty of brave Israelite warriors, it didn't take a genius to conclude that Shaq O'Neil wielding a sword would be a prohibitive underdog against that sort of bulk, power and wingspan. If those iron-smithing Philistines armed their champion with a height and weight appropriate bladed instrument, Goliath could cut an SUV in half with a single stroke. Goliath carried a spear as well—with which he could probably have made shish kabob of an elephant at 100 yards. So the waiting game continued.

Armies in the field, of course, need to be provisioned. So Jesse, David's father, called him from the fields and sent him to take supplies to his brothers in the army. When David arrived in camp, it did not take him long to get up to speed on the situation. Young David, possessed of courage, faith and an idea, volunteered to take on Goliath. Out there with the sheep, David had had a lot of time on his hands. He had apparently spent those idle hours in target practice mastering the sling—a weapon that he had used repeatedly in defense of the sheep.

Though initially reluctant to let the lad undertake the challenge, King Saul was at last persuaded. He attempted to send David sheathed with his own personal armor and sword, but the boy declined. Saul's armor was too heavy and cumbersome to give him freedom of movement. The kid, at least, had enough sense to know that if the combat got into close quarters Goliath would make minced carrion of him anyway. So David stepped out against Goliath unshielded and armed only with his sling and a handful of aerodynamically appropriate stones he scooped up from the riverbed.

Well, you know the outcome. There was a good deal of trash talking on both sides. Then David wound up his sling and let fly. He caught the Philistine champion right between the eyes and down Goliath went. David beheaded him with his own sword and carried the trophy back to King Saul. The Philistines retired from the field and David became a hero.

That's not the end of David's story, of course. Being a hero can become a burden after the cheers have faded. Saul became understandably jealous of David's celebrity and their falling out became something of a minor civil war. David ultimately succeeded Saul as king of Israel. He went on to have a long and checkered, but ultimately successful, reign. King David went on as well to have a number of wives, which in itself requires a certain kind of heroism. It's not surprising that later in life he was dogged with family problems, in large part of his own making.

As a king, however, David brought stability to the fledgling monarchy of Israel. A succession of military victories finally established the tiny nation's security and defined its borders. The country prospered. Through David's ups and downs as king, he maintained that bedrock faith in God which motivated his confrontation with Goliath.

In fact, he wrote poetry over a period of many years about his relationship with God in all the circumstances of his heroic life. His poems record his thanks to God for blessing, his self-doubt and moral weaknesses, his joy in life and in the wonders of the world, his lusts and ambition, his contrition and shame and an abiding gratitude for God's faithfulness to him. It's the most read poetry in the history of the world. We call David's poems *The Psalms*.

CHAPTER 4

King Arthur: The Hero of Romance

"In short, there's simply not / A more congenial spot
For happily ever—aftering than here in Camelot."

For almost 800 years, the legendary figure of King
Arthur has been synonymous with the idyllic and
noble ideals of chivalry, justice and a romantic longing
for a champion of the right. A vigilant warlord, Arthur
sought to use the power of his kingdom to better the
spiritual and physical lives of his people. That is still a
pretty revolutionary idea today.

Of course, things get fouled up when we talk about
ideals, and those ideals failed Arthur in the end. Hope
springs eternal, however, and that is part of Arthur's
enchantment. The real story of King Arthur, though, had
actually begun another 800 years earlier.

After the Roman Legions were withdrawn from Great
Britain in the 4th century, the Romanized Celts, who had
lived under Roman administration and culture for three

centuries, were left on their own. Two political parties emerged in Britain, a Nationalist party and an Imperial party. The Imperial party wished to remain a part of the Roman Empire, governed by Roman law and custom. The Nationalist party chose to revive Celtic law, custom and way of life. Lacking the central administration that Rome had provided, over a generation or two, Britain devolved into a loose alliance of regional Celtic kingdoms.

Into the island from the East came Germanic peoples, Saxons, Angles and Jutes, in need of *lebensraum*. The Anglo-Saxons did not pretend to an organized military invasion of Britain, they just moved in—and then pressed their expansion across Britain. Local British kings attempted to check the war-like advance of the Anglo-Saxons for a hundred years, forming and reforming petty alliances, and generally failing to present a united front as they were pushed bit by bit toward the western and northern extremities of the island.

Lo, and it came to pass that there arose in the kingdom of Powys a warlord whose *nom de guerre* was The Bear. He proved his heroic mettle on the battlefield in local skirmishes with the Saxon interlopers and when he became King of Powys and Gwynedd, succeeded in bringing together the disparate regional Celtic kingdoms from Cornwall to the Scottish Lowlands in common cause. The Bear united the Imperialist party and the Nationalist party and in a dozen battles fended off Anglo-Saxon encroachment into the west and north of Great Britain. From his capital city of Viroconium (near present-day Shrewsbury), Arthur presided over peace for a generation.

The 5th-century king of Powys was named Owain Ddantgwynn, but he became a legendary hero under his battle name. The Celtic noun for bear is *arth*; the Latin, *ursus*. He was King *Arthursis:* the Bear. No like hero has passed into such historical obscurity and yet become such a figure of iconic heroism. King Arthur is the quintessential romantic hero.

After Arthur's death in an internecine squabble, the alliance he had built dissolved. Subsequently, over the next century or so, the indigenous Brits were ineluctably pushed to the western and northern extremities of Britain— to Cornwall, Wales and Scotland. The rest of Britain had become Angle-land. But by the hearth fires of the suppressed Celtic peoples, they told wistful tales of Arthur the king and his golden age. One day, it was said, he would return to lead his people to glory.

Ah, what goes around comes around. In 1066, William, the Duke of Normandy came across the English Channel and whumped the Saxon king Harold Godwinson in a pitched battle at Battle, generally known as the Battle of Hastings. In one fell swoop he becomes William the Conqueror, and King of England. Over the next few years, he Normanized the country and the Anglo-Saxons become second-class citizens. Pretty soon, they borrow from the Celts the idea of King Arthur coming to save *them.*

Then, an Oxford monk known as Geoffrey of Monmouth wrote a book called *The History of the Kings of Britain*, which was more fiction than history, but drew upon the legends that had long been told about King Arthur. Soon after, a couple of other monks, Wace and Layamon, wrote *romans*, or verse stories about King Arthur, and a cottage industry was born. From the 13th to the 16th century, medieval Europe was inundated with romances of King Arthur. In every major European language, the story of the chivalrous king, his exploits and his vision was told, enhanced and retold. Every writer added their own embellishments and new tales to Arthur's fictional history. The culmination of this medieval Arthurmania was Sir Thomas Mallory's mammoth account of the story *La Morte D'Arthur* in 1456.

Since then, the popularity of the Arthurian saga has ebbed and flowed. King Henry VII named his first son Arthur in an attempt to capitalize on residual English sentiment and legitimize his assumption of the throne by conquest. Later, Arthurian romance enjoyed a great revival in Victorian times when Alfred, Lord Tennyson, high priest of Victorian poetry, wrote *The Idylls of the King* and nobles held jousting tournaments.

Today, King Arthur is as popular as ever. Writers as diverse as John Steinbeck, C.S. Lewis, T.H. White, Mary Stuart, Lerner & Lowe and Monty Python have tapped into the dream of a king who has all the knightly virtues and promotes a civic order of chivalric ideals and justice.

Whatever the personal attributes of the "historic" *Arth-ursis*, the King Arthur of medieval romance unites a people in a war of independence, brings righteousness to a kingdom and inspires the quest for the Holy Grail. That is a good resume for a hero. By his exploits and his ethos, however, King Arthur is the prototype of the knight in shining armor. He is chivalrous and courtly to the ladies, skilled and courageous in the arts of war, motivated to pursue the good rather than aggrandize himself and to use his power of authority for justice and the general welfare.

There *is* that business of Guinevere and Lancelot, of course, which might be summarized as his wife running off with his best friend. And then there is the civil war that brought about the downfall of Arthur and his kingdom. These bits do add poignancy to the story. But there could not be a happy-ever-after. That would have reduced the King Arthur romances to the level of fairy tale, and, then too, the Celtic Britons did not enjoy a happy ending to the summer of Arthur's reign among them.

The ways in which life in the early 21st century is qualitatively better than life in medieval Europe are too numerous to recount. The humblest cottager of today lives far more securely and comfortably than did any medieval noble. Medicine, sanitation, diet, plumbing and heating, transportation and communications of medieval times are unfathomable in our era of climate controlled environments, transcontinental flights and 5G internet.

Yet we retain a constant fascination with medieval life and tromp to Medieval Fayres to munch on turkey legs; we read modern romances set in a Plantagenet world; we make a good size market in faux medieval baubles, decorations and potions. What draws us is our attraction to the world of King Arthur, the romantic hero.

We retain a longing for a world where political power is welded to a passion for creating a just society. Add a bit of a love interest, a dash of mysticism and a touch of a sexy edge, and there you have it: King Arthur and Camelot.

CHAPTER 5

William Wallace: The Tribal Hero

"When I was a boy, the priest, my uncle, carefully inculcated upon me this proverb, which I then learned and have ever since kept in my mind: 'I tell you a truth: Liberty is the best of things, my son; never live under any slavish bond.'"

Almost 800 years after William Wallace led his populist revolt against the feudal overlordship of England, Wallace is still the archetypal emblem of Scottish nationalism. Though Scotland had a national border and king for many centuries before Wallace's crusade against the England of Edward I in 1282, the country existed primarily as a collection of clans—a shifting montage of regional and family alliances. Serving the clan, its loyalties and its interests always held preeminence over any broader national interest.

One of the reasons why Americans have such a difficult time understanding the cultural and political dynamic of Europe (and the rest of the world, for that matter) is that we do not understand the concept of tribe. Apart from those Native Americans who have maintained a clear sense of tribal identity, we have no *gestalt* on a country carved or molded from peoples whose primary identity is tribal rather than national. From Puget Sound to Penobscot Bay, Americans may feel a sense of loyalty and identity with their locality, state and region. There is no question, however, that our primary sense of social identity is as Americans rather than as Jayhawks and Tarheels, New Yorkers or Californians.

Much as Mel Gibson did to raise contemporary consciousness of Wallace in the great movie *Braveheart*, it will come as no shock to discover that the film depiction of Wallace's life and times departed significantly from the historical reality. For instance, it was the Picts whom Roman historians recorded as painting their bodies blue for battle. That was a dozen centuries before Wallace, though, and the Picts had long been assimilated into the clans of the Scots. To paint lowland Scots of the 13th century that way for battle was anachronistic by a thousand years. It just goes to show what a difficult time the Scots have had gaining respect for their national identity through the ages. It's been tough living in the shadow of England all through history. That's what Wallace found.

William Wallace was born around 1270 in Ayrshire. His father was a knight and Laird of Elderslie and Auchinbothie, a figure of minor gentry. Though little is factually known of Wallace's youth, it's believed he was educated in French and Latin by his uncles near Stirling. He would have also trained in horsemanship and martial arts. Far from being a peasant or a crofter, Wallace had the upbringing and advantages of the Scottish nobility. Contemporary accounts say that Wallace was six and a half feet tall (at a time when most men were about 5'). His body was described as well-proportioned and he was renowned for his agility of body and fleetness of foot.

When King Alexander III died in 1286, Scotland was thrown into a contested succession, with a baker's dozen of the Scottish nobility putting forward a claim to the throne. There were several serious contenders and the claimants put the question to England's King Edward I for arbitration. At the time, Scotland was broadly occupied by England. To Edward and the English they were a vassal state that owed him feudal submission. Edward arrived at the Borders with a large army and ultimately forced the homage of each potential king. In 1292, Edward picked John Balliol as monarch, who swore an oath of fealty as vassal to Edward.

But these were times of lawlessness. English troops and mercenaries marauded the countryside from their castles and stockades, while Scottish nobles did little to maintain law. In 1291, Wallace's father was killed in a skirmish with the English, enflaming a lifelong desire in the young Wallace for a Scotland that was free from and rid of the English. From that time, Wallace lived as an outlaw, moving from place to place, recruiting men to his side and launching small-scale guerilla attacks against the hated English minions.

As Wallace's reputation spread, he gained support and broadened his attacks. In May 1297, with a party of 30 men, he ambushed and killed the English Sheriff of Lanarkshire, the knight responsible for his father's death seven years earlier. By now, Wallace found himself as a rallying point for a growing Scottish revolt against English overlordship. After several victorious battles through the summer, Wallace combined forces with a rebel army led by Andrew Moray to march on the strategically important stronghold of Stirling Castle. At the Battle of Stirling Bridge, September 1297, Wallace led a vastly outnumbered amateur army of Scots against the Earl of Surrey's 300 armored cavalry and 10,000 trained infantry. Wallace lured the English army into committing itself to crossing the narrow bridge. His ragtag army of peasants and small landowners made a killing field of the bottleneck. The English force became divided by the River Forth. Wallace had sent a second force across the river further upstream that attacked the English from its rear, pushing them in a crush to the river.

It was a spectacular victory for Wallace, unprecedented in centuries of Scottish conflict against England's superior wealth and resources, leaving 5,000 English dead upon the field. Wallace had shown himself to be not only a charismatic warlord, but a cunning military tactician. He was knighted thereafter, it is said, by Robert the Bruce, and he was declared Guardian of the Kingdom. The next summer, the English invaded in force.

After several months of seeking to bring Wallace to battle, Edward I caught up with Wallace's army at Falkirk. In the battle that followed, English longbowmen decimated the schiltrons of Scottish warriors armed with their axes and broadswords. Thousands of Scots died in defeat at the Battle of Falkirk, and Wallace escaped into the hills. The Bruce became Guardian of the Kingdom and made a temporary Scottish peace with Edward in

1302. But Wallace continued to elude English capture and disappears from history for several years.

A Scottish knight in Edward's service betrayed Wallace in August 1305 and he was captured near Glasgow. Wallace was carted south to London and put on trial in Westminster. The charge was treason and he was condemned as a traitor to the king. As William Wallace rightly protested, however, he had never sworn allegiance to England: "I could not be a traitor to Edward, for I was never his subject."

William Wallace was executed on August 23, 1305, dragged naked by the heels to Smithfield Market where he was hung, drawn and quartered. His head was impaled on London Bridge, his body quarters displayed in Newcastle, Berwick, Aberdeen and Perth. Wallace's martyrdom for Scottish independence lit the fire. Robert the Bruce revived the Scottish rebellion, sealed Scottish independence with the Arbroath Declaration and was crowned king in 1306.

Ultimately, Wallace won, and won for himself a rare immortality as an iconic hero of Scottish identity.

CHAPTER 6

Joan of Arc: The Visionary Hero

"One life is all we have and we live it as we believe in living it. But to sacrifice what you are and to live without belief, that is a fate more terrible than dying."

In classical terms, the warrior hero was a man. Back in Greek and Roman times a woman, such as Helen of Troy, might inspire warfare and heroic deeds, but women were rarely in the kind of battlefield position where ancient heroes were made.

There was Bodicea, of course. She was the warrior queen of the Iceni tribe, the Celts of East Anglia. Bodicea led the most famous revolt against the Romans in the four-century history of their occupation of Great Britain. She was a wild combat warrior who led her Celtic armies riding a chariot into the thick of battle. The Iceni army and their allies, however, were unsurprisingly no match for the disciplined Roman legionnaires. In the end, Bodicea went down to ignominious defeat and death, liberated no people and accomplished nothing. Not terribly heroic.

Of course, there were women of heroic deeds, virtues and accomplishments back in those centuries, but rarely were they recorded, and rarely recognized as heroic by the standards of the day. There are Biblical women, too, like Rahab, Esther and Deborah who model a heroic character, but hardly the classical idea of the laurelled warrior. In the 1400s, however, along came a girl who would change history in more ways than one.

Joan of Arc was born a peasant in the French village of Domremy, Lorraine in 1412. D'Arc was her family name, not an honorific title of some kind. As a girl of 12, she began to report visions of early Christian saints and of St. Michael the Archangel, patron saint of the French army.

France and England had been warring for decades. Now, a civil war between factions of the French royal family, the Orleanists and the Burgundians, had brought an English invasion under Henry V who claimed the French throne for himself with Burgundian backing. By 1428 much of France, including Paris, was under English control. The situation was desperate for Charles, Duke of Orleans, and the French cause.

For several years, the visions Joan received of Saints Catherine and Margaret had been calling her to go to the Royal Court and convince the Duke that God wanted her to lead an army against the English and Burgundians. After much persistence, Joan succeeded in having the local commander deliver her through enemy territory to Charles's court in Chinon. There, she told the Duke: "I am come and am sent in the name of God to bring aid to you and to the kingdom."

In truth, the Orleanist cause was about lost. Orleans was under English siege, and the treasury was empty. Everything militarily had been tried to hold the Burgundians and their English allies at bay. That the court would entertain to even listen to the apparently outlandish claims of a village peasant girl is a mark of how desperate the situation was seen to be. Still, out of either desperation or inspiration, Charles felt he had little to lose. The story is that Joan convinced Charles to listen by telling him of a personal prayer he had prayed months before.

After Charles had Joan examined for three weeks by theologians of the University of Paris, he was apparently convinced that Joan did indeed bring providential aid to his cause. Joan d'Arc was fitted with full body armor and given titular command of the French army at Blois. She carried before the army a banner with a picture of Christ holding up the world on a white background spangled with gold fleurs-de-lis.

As the dispirited French army moved to relieve the siege of Orleans, volunteers joined the campaign as word spread that a saint was at the head of the army. With Joan carrying her banner into battle, she spurred French soldiers to tenacious assaults on the city. The English abandoned the siege after repeated French attack. The breaking of the siege reversed Charles's fortunes and several prominent nobles and clerics rallied to his side.

The Maid of Orleans, as she became known, convinced the Duke to march the army north through English and Burgundian-held territory to Reims, where French kings were traditionally crowned in Reims Cathedral. To open the way to a northern front, the army first had to clear the

English out of the Loire Valley. In a matter of days, Joan inspired French victories at Jargeau, Beaugency and Patay.

The walled towns of medieval France opened before Charles and his army as they made their way north to Reims. During the Duke's coronation as King Charles VII, Joan stood beside him with her banner. After the crowning, Joan told him: "Now is accomplished the pleasure of God, who wished me to lift the siege of Orleans and to bring you to this city of Reims to receive your holy anointing." Then, the cheeky girl sent a letter to the Duke of Burgundy asking why he didn't show up for the coronation.

The war continued to drag on, as medieval wars did, and the French armies advanced; Joan continued for two years to lead soldiers into combat. In May 1430, however, she was apparently betrayed, ambushed by Burgundian forces at Compiegne and taken captive. Her capture devastated the Orleanists and predictably overjoyed their enemies. Though Charles VII made efforts to ransom the Maid, the Burgundians refused and subsequently handed her over to the English.

Joan was brought to the English seat at Rouen and put on trial in a court of the Inquisition for heresy. To simply kill her would not be sporting. As it was customary at the time to put heretics to death by burning them at the stake with the blessing of the Church and almost everyone else, this seemed a convenient way of disposing of Joan. After all, that Joan claimed to have visions and voices from God was public knowledge. Such a claim was an *ipso facto* admission of heresy. Besides that, she sometimes dressed in men's clothing. The show trial with a stacked court of English-favoring clerics was something of a judicial farce lasting five weeks. Joan defended herself against the clerical inquisition with intellect and subtlety. The conclusion, though, was predictably foregone. Joan of Arc was burned at the stake as a condemned heretic in March 1431.

When the English abandoned Rouen in 1449, her case was appealed. The Inquisitor acquitted her posthumously and determined that Joan was a martyr. In 1920, the shepherd girl from the French outback was canonized, St. Joan of Arc.

Like any other national, military and spiritual hero, Joan has her detractors. If Lord Nelson was no hero to the French, Joan of Arc was no hero to the English. And visions and voices from God are always going to make some people believers, some people skeptics and some people scared. It does not matter; what Joan did was real. She led armies in successful combat; she inspired a new nationalism in the beleaguered people of her nation; she was the motive force in the coronation of Charles VII as King of France. She died a tortured and shameful death unjustly even by the standards of medieval warfare.

Through the centuries, Joan of Arc has continued to inspire generations of soldiers who have fought on French soil. Perhaps far more importantly, however, Joan became the first classic heroine. By her life, she told peasant girls everywhere that they, too, could accomplish great things.

CHAPTER 7

Captain James Cook: The Explorer Hero

"Do just once what others say you can't do, and you will never pay attention to their limitations again."

That the world is a scary place falls into the category of a truism. Yes, there are those who manage to swagger through existence without seeming to acknowledge their own vulnerability and fragility in the world. Most of us, though, harbor fears and phobias of one kind or another whether they be rational or not. Fear of heights, fear of flying, fear of hypodermic needles, the dentist's chair or enclosed spaces: there is certainly no shortage of elements and experiences in the world that can delimit our quality of life and drive our decisions.

Our greatest fear, however, and that which touches on all the rest is fear of the unknown. A good therapist and better living through chemistry can mitigate many fears, but nothing can relieve our dread of the unknown.

The courage to act in the face of fear of the unknown is among the most impressive qualities of heroism. Such courage is a necessary strength of character in those who are explorers of land, sea and space. True explorers are a pretty rare breed these days. Many of us don't even know what darkness is—living in a lit-up electric-powered world of streetlights and nightlights of all varieties. We cannot even imagine the darkness of setting forth into a physical world unknown. The reality is there just isn't much of the globe left to really explore. Much of this country's population lives where there are airplanes in the sky overhead day and night.

From the 16th to 18th centuries, however, exploring was all the rage and explorers were superstars of their day. Setting off across uncharted waters on voyages of discovery was not an easy undertaking nor one for the timid of heart.

From virtually every European coastal country sailors set out to discover new lands, seeking riches and glory, and political and geographical advantages for their home nations. Wooden vessels of the era were small and cramped and driven only by the fickle and unpredictable power of the wind. Navigation was primitive and unreliable; foodstuffs were basic, their quantity finite and their nutritional value woefully incomplete; communication with home was nonexistent. The length of voyages was always uncertain, but well apt to take captain and crew away from the known world for two or three years. Ferdinand Magellan, Vasco De Gama, John Cabot, Francis Drake, Henry Hudson and more: the names of these men are recalled in place names throughout the Western Hemisphere and the South Pacific.

Captain James Cook is not much known in this part of the world. In Australia and New Zealand, though, Captain Cook is the rough equivalent of Christopher Columbus. He might not actually have been the first European to potter about some of those parts, but he literally put them on the map. A good many folk who know about these things regard Cook as the greatest of all in the age of explorers.

Born in North Yorkshire in 1728 near what is now Middlesbrough, Cook came from a humble family of farm laborers. After an unsuitable apprenticeship to a grocer, Cook ended up as a teenager in the harbor town of Whitby and signed on as merchant seaman in the coal trade, plying coal down the coast from Yorkshire and Northumbria to London. In the process, he taught himself the skills of navigation: algebra, trigonometry and astronomy.

In 1755, with Britain arming for the Seven Years War (of which the French and Indian War was one theater), Cook left the merchant navy for military service, beginning as an able seaman aboard HMS *Eagle*. His talent for surveying and cartography was put to good service in the western North Atlantic. He mapped much of the St. Lawrence estuary, allowing General Wolfe to lay the siege of Quebec. Later, he spent five years surveying Atlantic Canada, producing the first accurate charts of the coast of Newfoundland.

Cook's successes brought him significant acclaim from the Royal Society and the Admiralty. In 1768, Cook was given command of *HM Endeavour* and sent to the Pacific Ocean to observe a rare transit of Venus across the Sun. Though sailors for centuries had been able to measure latitude with a sextant, determining longitude was much more complex. Recording the transit of Venus from different points around the globe would provide the astral measurements that would make calculations of longitude infinitely more accurate.

Having completed that assignment, however, Cook was then charged with prowling around the South Pacific in search of an unknown southern continent referred to for centuries as *Terra Australis*. In the process, he became the second European to reach New Zealand and mapped the complete New Zealand coastline, discovering in the process Cook Strait, which separates the two principal islands of the country.

Moving west, Cook struck the southeastern tip of Australia, becoming the first European to see the east coast of that continent. The *Endeavour* sailed north, with Cook charting the coast naming the landmarks along the way. By the time Cook returned home in 1771, he had been gone three years. The space shuttle *Endeavor* was named for his ship.

Though the publication of Cook's journals brought him a certain amount of celebrity, it was thought that he had failed to find *Terra Australis*. Despite Australia's obviously being a continent-sized land mass, the putative southern continent was judged to be further south. The next year he was sent to try again, this time commanding the *Resolution*. He became among the first to cross the Arctic Circle and circumnavigated the globe around the Antarctic continent. Before returning home from his second three-year voyage, Captain Cook had put Easter Island, Vanuatu, South Georgia, the South Sandwich and Friendly Islands on the map.

Captain Cook set out a third time in 1776, again in *Resolution*. By now, the myth of *Terra Australis* had been largely laid to rest, but much of the Pacific was still unknown. Sailing north from Tahiti, Cook became the first European to set foot in Hawaii (which he named the Sandwich Islands after the First Lord of the Admiralty). Then, he traveled east to the west coast of North America. He charted the coast from California north to the Bering Strait, in search of another long-sought-for geographical fiction—the Northwest Passage. On his return to Hawaii in 1779, a contretemps with the natives resulted in Cook's death at their hands.

It would have been nice had Cook been able to live long enough to enjoy the accolades his accomplishments deserved, but those are the chances he took. That he was willing to brave the unknown resulted in almost a third of the world becoming known. That's a pretty impressive legacy.

Now days it is a tough world for those with the soul of an explorer-adventurer. Our ongoing attempts to break the bounds of earth provide some few astronauts with the rush: Alan Shepherd, John Glen, Neil Armstrong—and Christa MacAuliffe. Lacking the *Golden Hind* or the *Endeavour* to command, adventurers sublimate today spelunking, scuba diving, rock climbing, or committing a summer to their 13-year-old daughter's softball team.

No, none of us today can imagine sailing off for untold years into an unknown world the way Captain James Cook did. The adventurer within us, though, is a heroic virtue to be embraced. After all, in one form or another, all human progress has depended on that longing to explore the unknown.

CHAPTER 8

Winston Churchill: The National Hero

"We make a living by what we get, but we make a life by what we give."

One day Winston Churchill was in his study working on a speech when his young grandson sneaked into the room and approached Churchill's desk. As the old statesman looked up, the boy asked, "Is it true what they say, Grandpa, that you are the greatest man in the world?" "Yes," Churchill barked, "Now bugger out of here!"

It takes history to become a national hero—a matter of destiny as well as character. To prove that a crime has been committed, the prosecutor presents a case that proves the miscreant had means, motive and opportunity. Likewise, for a person to become a national hero it takes time, place and character. Being caught in the flux of history; being in the right place at the right time; and knowing that destiny placed you there.

To be a national hero is to be embraced with affection and revered memory across a broad cross-section of society. Across the gamut of partisan affections and subcultures within a country, the confluence of time and place creates an icon of national identity and national pride. In reality, there are few genuine national heroes in world history—at least in the league with such as George Washington, Joan of Arc, Simon Bolivar, Moses and Pele.

Each of them had within the heart of a hero: tenacity, the willingness to make hard decisions, courage in adversity and the humility to take responsibility. At the same time, it is not these characteristics alone in a person that elevates them in the eyes of history.

In now barely living memory, there is perhaps no clearer example of the national hero than Winston Churchill. An extensive BBC poll a few years back identified Churchill as the Greatest Briton of All Time in the hearts of the British people.

Statesman and soldier, master politician and Nobel prize-winning author, few if any left a stronger mark upon the 20th century than Churchill. His bulldog determination and confidence as wartime prime minister rallied the British people and inspired and directed their against-all-odds struggle with the European Nazi empire.

By the time Churchill became prime minister in 1940, he had already enjoyed a full career in Parliament and in the Cabinet, including turns in office as First Lord of the Admiralty, Home Secretary, President of the Board of Trade and Chancellor of the Exchequer. He was already old enough to retire with honors.

From the beginning, Churchill *wanted* the glory. He loved the adventure and the limelight. As a youth,

Churchill had been a celebrated war correspondent in the Boer War, famously having escaped captivity from the Afrikaaners. He took a turn as a combat army officer in the colonial wars and came back to stand for Parliament.

Churchill was irascible and confident, brusque and impatient. His consumption of cigars and brandy alone would probably keep him out of polite society today. After serving in a variety of ministerial capacities from World War I through the 1920s, Churchill spent a good part of the 1930s in enforced political retirement at his Kent home, Chartwell. He called these his "wilderness years." He took up painting and gardening in part to distract himself from the gray clouds of inactivity looming over him—and from the gray clouds of Fascism increasingly threatening Britain from the Continent. Churchill became a needling thorn in the side of successive weak Governments in his call for British rearmament in the face of rising Nazi militarism.

When war was made inevitable by Germany's invasion of Poland in 1939, it was not long before the conciliatory Government of Neville Chamberlain collapsed. It became a question of national survival more than party politics to find the right wartime prime minister. Churchill had 30 years of experience in Parliament and Whitehall, and he had been one of the few public voices who had warned of what was to come in Europe. Beyond that, Churchill wanted the job. Like that fire-in-the-belly basketball player who wants the ball when the game is on the line, Churchill wanted the shot. And he got it.

After King George VI summoned him to the palace and asked him to form a wartime government, Churchill wrote: "I felt as if I were walking with destiny, and that all my past life had been but a preparation for this hour and this trial."

The new prime minister weighed into the job with the kind of focus that comes with confidence. Assembling a non-party wartime cabinet, Churchill directed every avenue of military preparation and home front operations. He was a hands-on military strategist and a tireless administrator. Britain had to be kept armed, fueled, fed and funded as it stood alone against the Nazi axis on the Atlantic wall of Europe. For all Winston Churchill actually *did* to achieve ultimate Allied victory in World War II, however, it is for unexcelled cheerleading that he is actually most remembered.

It is sadly impossible for us to imagine today the emotional, mental and physical strain that the British people lived under during the long months of the Battle of Britain and the hard years before America entered the war. They suffered the casualties of a 9/11 event every night for months as Luftwaffe pilots bombed cities from the Clyde to Cornwall. Young British lads in their teens and 20s by the thousands died in the RAF defense of the island. The British people lived with dispiriting rationing of all kinds of goods, constant fear, life-consuming effort and pervasive grief. And Churchill led them to victory.

In bully pulpits from the House of Commons to the BBC, Churchill rallied the spirits and the efforts of the nation. With bombs raining down nightly on London, the prime minister inspired the people on to their own heroic and historic efforts—on to "their finest hour." Churchill himself became the personification of Britain's determination to win glory for themselves. Portly, proud and petulant, Churchill was indeed a physical embodiment of John Bull.

Winston Churchill's dramatic and heroic wartime leadership takes center stage in his life story. When he was replaced as prime minister by a war-weary nation, however, he continued to lead the Conservative Party for another 10 years, well into his 80s; he returned to become a Cold War prime minister from 1951-55. He won the Nobel Prize for writing the six-volume *The Second World War* and penned his four-volume masterpiece *A History of the English Speaking People.*

When Churchill left government for the last time in 1955, his son Randolph wrote to him: "Your glory is enshrined forever on the unperishable plinth of your achievement . . . It will flow with the centuries." In many ways, the same thing can be said of all those who are heroes, however acclaimed or obscured from public view. Of few individuals, however, can it be said whose achievements were on a larger stage of history, or whose contribution will be so widely known by it.

While the great man had an ego not to be denied, Churchill always affirmed that it was the British people, not himself, who brought them through the fires of WWII. As he wrote years later: "It was the nation and the race dwelling all round the globe that had the lion's heart. I had the luck to be called upon to give the roar."

Certainly Winston Churchill had that lion's heart of a hero. He was a swashbuckling risk-taker, with no self-doubt about him, and no doubt about the righteousness of the war he helped directed to its victorious conclusion. He made life and death decisions every day and lived with the responsibility; he evinced no apparent fear putting himself in harm's way.

At the same time, had world events turned out differently, Churchill might have spent the last 30 years of his life building stone walls and painting landscapes at

Chartwell, just another colorful career politician in the annals of British government.

Few of us will be Churchills in scope of fame and influence. But heroes live amongst us unawares, whose heart is there, and whose time and place are yet to come.

CHAPTER 9

Douglas MacArthur: The Warrior Hero

"It is my hope that my son, when I am gone, will remember me not for the battle, but in the home repeating with him our simple daily prayer, 'Our Father who art in heaven.'"

The ancient concept of the powerful, commanding warrior hero is rather dim now in our public consciousness. Perhaps this is a good thing. It means we have not had a theater of world events necessary to bring them to our attention. Lord knows that could change at any time. The generation now nearly past is the last to remember such heroes. Montgomery, Patton, Halsey, Merrill: World War II produced a fair share of courageous, battle-hardened commanders. George Patton even believed that he was the reincarnation of a Roman general. Surely, if the classic warrior hero exists in dimly lit memory, though, it must be Douglas MacArthur.

Like so many of our heroes, MacArthur was controversial in his lifetime and is hardly universally admired today. After all, he had a military heart, a military mind and he bled khaki.

Douglas MacArthur never knew anything in life but the United States Army, recalling famously, "My first memory was the sound of bugles." Born into a military family in 1880, MacArthur's father was a career officer and Congressional Medal of Honor winner in the Civil War. Throughout his early years, MacArthur and his family followed his father's postings across the Southwest and to Washington. After school at the West Texas Military Academy, MacArthur entered West Point, graduating first in his class in 1903 with one of the finest records in academy history. He was commissioned into the Corps of Engineers.

Like all young officers, MacArthur's early career saw a variety of assignments. His lifelong connection with the Philippines began with an early posting to the islands. He also did a tour of Asia as an aide to his father, General MacArthur, a stint as White House aide to Teddy Roosevelt and lackluster stays in the Midwest, before being posted to the War Department following the death of his father in 1912. He served on the War Department's general staff until American entry into World War I in 1917.

MacArthur went to France as chief of staff to the Rainbow Division, was promoted to the rank of brigadier general and commanded the 84th Infantry Brigade. He quickly became known as a swashbuckling hands-on commander, leading his troops into battle from the front (often without a weapon). In the process, MacArthur became the most decorated American soldier of the war, receiving two Purple Hearts, two Distinguished Service Crosses, seven Silver Stars and a Distinguished Service medal.

After the war, now General MacArthur became Superintendent of West Point. During his term at the Academy, MacArthur modernized the curriculum with the introduction of liberal arts and radically updated its program of officer preparedness to reflect the realities of 20th-century warfare. Through the 1920s, MacArthur served two tours in the Philippines and posts as corps commander in the States. In 1930, President Hoover appointed Douglas MacArthur Army Chief of Staff. His was the task of reorganizing the army administratively and accommodating it to the difficult years of the Great Depression. When the Philippines were heading to independence in 1935, Philippine President and long-time friend, Manuel Quezon, sought MacArthur's services to form and train a Philippine Army. President Roosevelt agreed and MacArthur returned to the Philippines.

If the story ended here, as well it might have, MacArthur would be one of American history's greatest generals—and few people would remember him. He actually retired from the Army in 1937, after 34 years of military service. He stayed on in the Philippines as a civilian advisor to the Philippine government. President Quezon, however, made him a Field Marshall of the Philippine Army. That's when he began wearing that famous field marshal's cap with the US Army crest.

In the middle of 1941, though, with war engulfing both Southeast Asia and Europe, Roosevelt recalled MacArthur to active duty as commander of US Armed Forces in the Far East. Through the Philippine campaign of 1941-42, MacArthur made headquarters on the island stronghold of Corregidor at the mouth of Manila Bay. As the Japanese juggernaut engulfed the Philippines, Roosevelt ordered

MacArthur out to the safety of Australia. With a handful of aides, his wife and young son, the General made a last-minute dash in a PT boat through the Japanese cordon.

When he arrived in Australia, MacArthur tossed down his gauntlet to the world with the famous words, "I came out of Bataan and I shall return." His words became a rallying cry for the war in the Pacific. For three long years MacArthur directed the bloody fighting through the archipelagos of Pacific islands. In October 1944, with the newsreel cameras rolling, the General waded ashore at Leyte and announced, "I have returned!" Over the next few months Allied forces liberated the rest of the Philippines. In 1945 MacArthur relocated his headquarters to Manila to plan the invasion of Japan. The bombing of Hiroshima and Nagasaki, of course, ended the war. MacArthur accepted the Japanese surrender aboard the *USS Missouri* on September 2nd.

With the fighting over, MacArthur was named Supreme Commander of the Allied Powers in Occupied Japan. In practice, that meant that he ran the country as military governor—and rebuilt it. Overseeing the reconstruction of Japan's infrastructure and economy, MacArthur effectively demilitarized and reorganized Japanese society and created the institutions of a modern democratic nation. The constitution MacArthur's staff drafted for Japan in 1946 remains today.

When MacArthur handed over power to a new Japanese government in 1949, it seemed again that his career might be over. In June 1950, however, the sudden outbreak of the Korean War, (which MacArthur termed "Mars' last gift to an old warrior"), brought MacArthur the command of American-led UN forces on the Korean peninsula. After the South Korean and UN troops had been driven south to a small area around Puson, MacArthur rallied a counter-offensive breaking out of the Puson Perimeter and launching a daring amphibious assault behind enemy lines at the Port of Inchon.

The success of MacArthur's troops in driving the North Koreans north into retreat brought the Chinese into the war as Chinese forces crossed the Yalu River and pushed the UN army south again. MacArthur wanted to take the war to the Chinese with the full power of American military might. President Truman, however, wanted to maintain a limited war confined to the Korean peninsula. MacArthur sounded off loudly and publicly. One hallmark of America's political stability, however, has always been civilian control of the military. MacArthur's vocal frustration amounted to insubordination, and in April 1951, Truman relieved MacArthur of command and recalled him home.

Last of the great World War II generals, MacArthur was greeted with a hero's welcome, a Manhattan tickertape parade and a televised farewell address to the joint Houses of Congress, where he essentially bowed from the public stage with his famous recollection: "Old soldiers never die, they just fade away." He lived quietly in retirement in New York until his death in 1964.

Unquestionably MacArthur was susceptible to a hero's vice—vanity. In its extreme, such pride can be hubris, the downfall of the *tragic* hero. Military triumph can be heady stuff. Julius Caesar, Napoleon, Nelson, Wellington, Patton and hoards of history's warriors can all attest. To commit and lead men into battle requires a special kind of narcissism. Sometimes the line between the hero and the tragic hero can be pretty thin. MacArthur flirted with ego-inspired controversy at several points during his long, accomplished career. At the end of the day, though, he knew where the buck stopped and what he fought for. That's a good valedictory for one of history's greatest warrior heroes.

CHAPTER 10

Don Quixote: The Quixotic Hero

"Fortune may have yet a better success in reserve for you, and they who lose today may win tomorrow."

Cervantes

To dream the impossible dream, to fight the unbeatable foe,
To bear with unbearable sorrow, to run where the brave dare not go.
To right the unrightable wrong, to love pure and chaste from afar,
To try when your arms are to weary, to reach the unreachable star.

......

And the world will be better for this:
That one man, scorned and covered with scars,
Still strove with his last ounce of courage,
To reach the unreachable stars.

Among the most endearing of characters in world literature is the loveable, dreamy and daft Don Quixote. The eponymous hero of Miquel Cervantes 17th-century comic epic is known today in popular culture as the knight errant brought to life in *The Man of La Mancha*, singing "The Impossible Dream."

Don Quixote brought into our language the adjective "quixotic," which means simply to be idealistic to an impractical degree. To be swept up by lofty romantic ideas, or extravagantly chivalrous activity. As a knight-errant, Quixote travels in search of adventures, to use his sword and lance to right wrongs, avenge injustices, serve the good and prove himself worthy of the lady he adores—Dulcinea.

Actually, our unprepossessing hero is Alonso Quijano, an aging hidalgo, a minor Spanish nobleman, who was obsessed with stories of chivalry and knight errantry. Friends and family think, with some reason, that he is nuts—to leave home on a seemingly goal-less quest, take the name Don Quixote de la Mancha and have himself knighted by an innkeeper.

Yes, Don Quixote travels the dusty countryside of Spain on his emaciated horse, Rocinante, accompanied by his faithful and comical squire, Sancho Panza. The old knight is dazed and confused in a world that has gone. He believes in the ideals of chivalry and courtly love, in a morality that did not exist in the contemporary world of the early 17th century and does not exist in ours.

Not only does Quixote live in a mythic and fictional past, his present is peopled with giants and enchantments. The lines between reality and imagination blur considerably in the old man. And the simple Sancho does his best to mediate between his master and the rest of the world. It is a mediation often needed. Despite the old knight's best intentions, his intervention against the perceived injustices of the world generally ends up making a mess of things. In practice, the world just is not as simple and black-and-white as he sees it.

In one of the novel's most famous scenes, Quixote envisions a battered windmill on the landscape as a malevolent giant and tilts his lance at its flapping sails. Predictably enough, charging a moving windmill on horseback with a lance proves to be a losing proposition. Quixote ends up ass-over-bandbox. To take on both a useless and ill-conceived cause to this day is known as "tilting at windmills."

At the heart of the chivalric code that Don Quixote strives to embody and defend is the convention of courtly love. This convention of the medieval romances the old hidalgo steeped in was a result of its times. Since back then no one worth knowing actually got *married* for love, it became fashionable in literature (and to some extent in real life) to promote a convention of idealized love—eh, ostensibly pure and chaste from afar. For sex itself, one generally resorted to the scullery maid, the barmaid or *in extremis* one's wife, to whom one may or may not have been physically attracted. For the emotion of romantic love, however, one idealized a woman, maiden or married, and devoted one's self and one's honor to this love—whether she reciprocated it or not. Or, for that matter, whether she was even aware of being the object of idealized passion or not. Yes, they had some strange social and sexual mores in those days, too.

In Don Quixote's case, the object of his love is an unattractive peasant lass, Aldonza Lorenzo. Quixote concludes she must be a beautiful princess under an evil enchantment. For her honor and in pursuit of her love, Quixote risks life and limb intervening where he does not belong.

Readers who are only familiar with our Spanish hero through *The Man of La Mancha* may be surprised to learn that Dulcinea, Aldonza Lorenzo, never actually appears in Cervantes' novel. The peasant girl to whom Quixote pledges his love and honor is an idealization always out of sight and out of reach.

The great George Balanchine choreographed *Don Quixote* into a ballet in 1965 with music by Nicolas Nabakov. In Balanchine's interpretation of our hero, he observed: "... everything man does he does for his ideal woman." Though our social rites and relationships are far removed from those of medieval romance, perhaps there is here a timeless truth.

For all his failures and lack of a full deck, Don Quixote remains an exemplar of heroic virtues. Courage is no less courage because the cause that activates it is not to our understanding or a cause popular with our peer group. That the billowing windmill is not in fact a giant to our perception does not diminish the courage it called forth in an old man to take arms against it.

One of the great motifs of literature is the difference between appearance and reality. In the real world, Don Quixote has trouble distinguishing between the two. At the same time, his life and quest reveal that the world—our own society as much as his—confuses appearance and reality in many ways. Quixote shows us that there is a big difference between socially prescribed codes of honor and personal honor. Sometimes doing the honorable thing can seem crazy in the eyes of the world. Personal honor, however, cannot be put in the balances by public opinion.

There is a difference as well between social appearance and reality. Cervantes' novel was a ground-breaking book at the time because it introduced the outlandish concept that a person's social class and their worth were not the same thing. Back in the 17th century, it was not polite to recognize that nobles are not necessarily noble and peasants necessarily inferior in wisdom, virtue and intellect. In objects and actions as well as in people, there is often a difference between true worth and perceived value.

No, it is not a profitable or prudential thing to set off from home and leave behind the responsibilities of one's life to pursue visionary idealism and hallucinogenic objectives; even Jimmy Buffett would agree. But there are times when the only way to be an honorable person is to strive against injustice regardless of the hopelessness of the cause, or to take life choices that the world does not understand.

History's annals are crowded with inventors and medical researchers, explorers and crusaders for justice at whom the world scoffed. On the other hand, many people live their whole lives without doing anything that would risk the good opinion of others. Generally, they are the ones who do nothing constructive or interesting with their lives at all.

CHAPTER 11

Robin Hood: The Folk Hero

"Essentially, Robin Hood put a smackdown on the medieval equivalent of the IRS."

Steven Crowder

A h, no search for the faces of heroism could be complete without including the uncrowned king of Sherwood Forest—Robin Hood. Apart from his general legendary exploits tweaking the nose of the Norman ascendancy like the Sheriff of Nottingham, Sir Guy of Gisborne and Prince John, the unique and lasting element of the Robin Hood legend is the very practical and popular notion of robbing from the rich to give to the poor. The closer one approximates being on the receiving end of the exchange, the more attractive the proposition sounds. Of course, neither practical politics nor moral arguments are quite that simple.

In the late 12th century, England was indeed divided into two castes. The native Saxons, or "English," had been bested a century earlier by William, the Duke of

Normandy, at the Battle of Hastings. The crown went to him and history calls him William the Conqueror. In those days, to the victor *really* belonged the spoils, and the spoils went to William and his heirs in the form of Norman feudalism. Within a generation, lands and titles were largely stripped from the Saxon thanes and granted to Norman knights and barons to reward their following William into battle. From *their* standpoint, that is what they risked life and limb *for*.

To the Saxons, of course, this Norman ascendancy and the administration it spawned was a foreign occupation. Norman rule and Norman law were arbitrarily foisted upon them; their overlords spoke a foreign language; the knights, armaments and castles by which the Normans enforced their way were overwhelming and intimidating. By the time of the Crusades and the famous Plantagenet king Richard the Lionheart, the Saxons were getting pretty tired of being oppressed and paying taxes to support the lifestyle of their oppressors. When Richard got himself captured for ransom by the Duke of Austria, they *really* did not like the idea of footing the burden for his ransom. Into this historical context rides a hero of the occupied people who did not stem the tide of history—but who gave the Saxon peasants and yeomen something to cheer about.

A Saxon yeoman, Robin of Locksley, outlawed by the Normans, takes refuge in the vast undergrowth of Sherwood Forest. He gathers around him a motley gang of peasants and vagabonds who have similarly run afoul of Norman law or found its bondage intolerable. Across the East Midlands of Nottinghamshire and its environs, the Merrie Men of Robin Hood take the Saxon countryfolk under their protection, avenging Norman injustice and relieving the destitution of their condition. Robin and his troop live in Sherwood Forest outside of society, largely by natural law. They dine on the King's deer, the poaching of which constitutes a capital offense under the law of the land. They do indeed finance their existence and their social program by relieving cash and chattel from the Norman nobility and their lackeys.

Robin Hood himself is the natural leader of this band of good-hearted brigands. As such, understandably, he is a magnificent physical specimen, chivalrous in love and master of the sexy weapon of the era—the longbow. He exemplifies courage and daring, risking himself over and over again for others. His leadership of the Merrie Men is unchallenged and he administers justice on their behalf with mercy and good will. How can you not love this guy?

Robin Hood's heroism lies in something beyond his physical exploits. Robin and his Merrie Men of Sherwood represent something that our present society aspires to in spirit, but hasn't figured out how to properly articulate and integrate into our law and social consciousness: equity.

We take just pride in being a people who live under law. We are taught and properly internalize the importance of law, respect for law and the power of law over our lives. At the same time, though we know in theory that it is not necessarily so, society *functions* as if law and justice were the same thing. In Robin Hood, we find a hero who instantiates our longing for equity over law. He reminds us that law is to be descriptive of natural law and moral right and not prescriptive.

I took a drive a few years back following old Route 66 from Chicago to Santa Monica Boulevard. Anywhere from western Oklahoma to the Mojave, I often found myself on desolate road, where I-15 lay a few miles or a few hundred yards to the north or south of the legendary abandoned highway. Across the desert you could see for miles in any direction to the distant buttes and the 180 degree sky. I could drive for half an hour at a clip at 80 and never see another vehicle or a sign of human life. And there in the middle of the desert a rare and lonely intersection with a back road leading up into the hills would be a four-way stop. Lonely red metal lollipops stuck in the sand, left over from the years when Route 66 was the Mother Road of America.

At first, I stopped. 'Twas an instinct bred into me with respect for the law. The ludicrousness of the situation did finally dawn on me. Breaking from speed to a dead stop where I had clear visibility to infinity and no sign of vehicular traffic or sentient life forms may have been the legal thing to do, but it was stupid. Did I have a *moral* obligation to obey the law? Did I have a *social* obligation to obey the law? At last, I sailed on through with no more thought for the law than a Merrie Man in pursuit of a deer.

If by some fluke, my car had been observed from a lost police helicopter, my license read and a citation for failure to stop at a stop sign sent to my home address, I would have been legally liable. Being guilty, of course, I would be subject to the censure of the law. Would *justice* have been served? No, the whole thing would just be silly.

In practice, though, while the judge herself or himself may have some latitude in determining my legal penalty, they would have leeway to adjudge whether I was or was not out-law. My violation of the law would go on my driving record and to my insurance company. It was the law itself that created the injustice. After all, in neither our civil nor our criminal courts do we charge judges with determining what is *fair*. We charge them with administering *law*. Neither common sense nor equity trump the law.

In an ideal world, the law would be a perfect tool for the administration of justice. In American society that is the deeply respected ideal, but it is far from perfect. The canyon between equity and justice is quite trivial when we are talking about a rusty stop sign somewhere in the Arizona desert. Throughout our society there are huge gulfs between law and equity that with all our good intentions we have not been able to erase. The law puts people in prison who should not be there and burdens individuals and all manner of institutions with taxation and regulation in ways that equity would not.

In Robin Hood, equity finds its champion. Back in 12th-century England, the gulf between law and equity was wide and uneven, its consequences far from trivial. In fact, equity was explicitly not the goal of society's lawmakers and law enforcers.

Perhaps unlike the good King Arthur, the Robin Hood legends may not derive from a historic individual who actually embodied the characteristics and led such a band in Sherwood during Prince John's regency. Several candidates for the "real" Robin Hood have been advanced over the years, but in the largest sense it certainly does not matter.

History or legend, Robin is a hero with heart and a champion of the underdog. Like such purely fictional characters as Zorro or the Scarlet Pimpernel, Robin Hood sees that right is done when right is outside the law.

CHAPTER 12

Jeanne Mance: The Medical Hero

The Angel of Ville-Marie

In the march of civilization and scientific progress over the last century, few areas of human life have benefited more than the field of medical knowledge and health care. Healers, however, have always been revered. It is intrinsically a calling of service to others. From the days of Doctor Kildare to the Good Doctor, television has turned out a steady stream of shows featuring doctors, nurses and hospitals. Like westerns, courtroom dramas and police shows, it's always easy to figure out who the good guys are. Like teaching, coaching and faith ministry, the healing professions are fertile earth for the seeds of heroism.

As in any profession or arena of life, however, it is not merely accomplishment that defines heroism. Millions of lives have been saved and for countless the quality of life has been immeasurably improved by medical research over the last half dozen decades. That is professionalism, though, on the part of university faculty and drug-company scientists, not heroism.

We get a little closer to the mark with Edward Jenner. The English country doctor noticed that milkmaids seemed prophylactically protected against the scourge of smallpox. Putting 2 and 14 together, Jenner developed an effective smallpox vaccine, and in a little shed in his garden freely (if crudely by contemporary standards) vaccinated all the local poor folk who came by. The value to humanity of Jenner's patient discovery is incalculable, as are those of medical researchers like Alexander Fleming, whose discovery in a petri dish led to penicillin, and Jonas Salk, who developed the vaccine for polio. Albert Schweitzer, Madame Curie, Florence Nightingale: there are any number of legendary figures in the field.

For a hero, we cast our eye for someone who sacrificed in service to the healing of others. Someone like Canadian pioneer Jeanne Mance.

Yes, it is true, I'm afraid. Americans are very good at taking Canada for granted. Even our television weather forecasts draw a line between Montana and Maine and rarely stray north. Since many of us can't find South Dakota on the map, most haven't got a prayer of locating New Brunswick. It always comes as a bit of a surprise to Yanks when we learn we were not first at something. The first hospital in the New World, however, was not established in Boston or Philadelphia, but in New France.

Jeanne Mance was a nurse, born in Langres in 1606, in France's Champagne region. As a girl she saw her town ravaged repeatedly by war and disease. Devout and caring, Mance dedicated herself to healing and became a nurse in the Thirty Year's War. In 1639, she was inspired by stories of three Ursuline sisters who had gone to New France to found a school for native girls. With the encouragement of a wealthy woman's support, Mance determined to go to Canada.

Mance joined the small party of 40 colonists under Paul Maisonneuve intent on founding a settlement upriver from Quebec. She became nurse, quartermaster and treasurer of the company. In May 1641 they set sail for New France. After wintering over in Quebec, the party moved up the St. Lawrence and founded Ville-Marie, modern Montreal, in 1642. Jeanne organized a dispensary and began caring for colonists and Algonquin natives. In 1645 she supervised construction of the Hotel Dieu, a 60 foot by 24-foot clapboarded log building—the first hospital in the New World. It became her life's work.

Montreal was a rough place in its early years. Harsh winters (with no Underground City), prevalent sickness and ever-present hostility with the violent Iroquois made the frontier community dangerous and deadly. Often Jeanne was caught in battle and several times narrowly escaped capture. But into Hotel Dieu, the gritty, compassionate woman welcomed the sick and wounded, settlers or natives. Amid the struggles of the young colony, Mance took in orphans and planted medicinal herb gardens.

Three times Mance returned to France, tirelessly raising funds for the hospital and the colony and recruiting workers to serve at Hotel Dieu. When Jeanne Mance returned to France the second time in 1659, she had been suffering for almost two years with a badly fractured arm. Accounts record that while praying at Saint Surplice in Paris on February 2, 1659, Jeanne's arm was cured. Three nuns of the Hospital Sisters of St. Joseph returned to Montreal with her to take up the work of the hospital.

On her last visit back to France in 1662, Jeanne had the foresight to provide a legal framework for Hotel Dieu's continued existence after her passing. Jeanne Mance gradually retired from her work, worn out from 30 years of tending the infant settlement's sick and wounded. She died in 1673 after a long illness and was buried in the hospital chapel at Hotel Dieu in relative obscurity.

In 1696, fire destroyed the hospital building and the remains of Jeanne Mance. Though she became largely forgotten, however, Hotel Dieu was rebuilt. The institution relocated in 1861 from the island of Ville Marie to the foot of Mount Royal. Hotel Dieu remains one of Montreal's premier hospitals. Over its long history, there have been many medical firsts at the New World's first hospital, including the world's first robotically-assisted laparoscopic surgery in 1993.

During Jeanne's lifetime, Montreal grew from a struggling colony of 40 settlers to a prosperous, stable town of 1,500. The unique presence of Jeanne Mance and her hospital from the settlement's beginning played a major role in that transformation. Montreal continued to grow, of course, and gradually Jeanne Mance has come to be recognized and acknowledged as co-founder of Montreal and one of Canada's great pioneer heroes.

Many kinds of heroism draw upon gifts that some of us have and some of us don't. Having the heart of a caregiver is such a gift. The medical arts are just that: arts. Healing is not simply the objective practice of applied medicine and pharmacology; from first-response Army medics in the killing fields of Iraq to those special nurses and underpaid aides who care for our elderly in nursing homes, and all those who have faithfully *cared* for the thousands of Covid-19 patients frightened and suffering in hospitals and care facilities, this is work that can only be done effectively from the heart.

In medicine as in so many fields, of course, women labored for centuries under the handicap of their gender. Jeanne Mance, nurse, would have had to wait two centuries before she could have done her serving as a credentialed doctor. That would take champions like Elizabeth Garrett Anderson, the first woman physician in Great Britain. In the mid-1800s, Elizabeth Garrett Anderson applied unsuccessfully to many medical schools. After private study, she passed the exam to get her apothecary license and opened a dispensary in London that became the New Hospital for Women and Children. Then, Anderson learned French in order to take the medical degree denied her in England at the Sorbonne in Paris. The British Medical Society admitted Anderson in 1873; she was the only woman member for 19 years. Jeanne Mance would have been so proud.

CHAPTER 13

Nathan Hale: Partisan Hero

"I wish to be useful, and every kind of service necessary to the public good becomes honorable by being necessary."

Not every martyr to a cause is a hero, and not everyone who gives their life for a cause heroically is motivated by religious belief or moral conviction. In the case of resistance to Nazism, it was easy to hold the political conviction, because the moral right was clear. There was no question in World War II who the good guys were. Any sedition, combat or sabotage against the aims and arms of the National Socialist state was intrinsically righteous. The moral right, however, is not always that clear in political conflict.

Many are the heroes of the American War of Independence; Francis Marion, Molly Pitcher, John Stark and George Washington come easily to mind. We could fill the page with the names of those who risked life and fortune in the cause of independence from Great Britain.

Their motives were not all the same, of course, but they shared a common goal.

With a unique approach to America history, David Hackett Fischer reveals in *Liberty and Freedom* that the New England colonies had a far different concept of a free people than did the Southern colonies. Later, these differing visions of American society would be contested, debated and compromised into the Constitution. Still later, of course, they would be contested in the War Between the States. There were those in 1776, however, who thought the place to debate differing visions of society to be the British Parliament.

It is easy to forget that there were tens of thousands of folks at that time who believed their moral duty lay with their king and established government. When war broke out between the Colonies and Britain, many people, particularly recently arrived colonists, returned to England. Other Loyalists sailed away from the Revolutionary tumult to the British colony in Nova Scotia, establishing Lunenburg as a safe haven for Tories fleeing the war. And many remained in cities like New York and Philadelphia, giving such support as they could to the embattled Redcoat armies of their mother country.

We hardly think of those colonial Loyalists today in heroic terms, if we think of them at all. Had the war for independence failed, however, as well it might have, we would be reading today about a very different set of heroes.

Wars have been fought throughout history for a variety of reasons, many of them abominable; the Revolutionary War was fought for a variety of reasons, many of them noble. There were no moral imperatives here, however, and conscience led colonists in both directions. Everyone was not even fighting for the same thing; many patriots fought for the independence of their own colony, not the establishment of a new nation. Neither the rabid colonists rebelling against their king and mother country nor the redcoat officers sent to quell their rebellion could claim of God's Providence that the "right" was on their side. Freedom (however it is perceived), though, is a great intoxicant and fired the belly of those we now call Patriots.

Nathan Hale, soldier hero of the American Revolution, was born in Coventry, Conn. in 1755. Nathan's father was a successful farmer, and sent Nathan and his brother Enoch to Yale College. When Hale graduated, at the age of 18, he accepted an appointment as the teacher of the Union Grammar School in New London, Conn. It was 1774 and the air was charged with the foment of rebellion. Hale joined the militia.

When the news of Lexington and Concord reached New London the next April, a town meeting was called. At this meeting, the young schoolteacher spoke: "Let us march immediately and never lay down our arms until we obtain our independence." Hale resigned his teaching position and was commissioned a First Lieutenant in the Seventh Connecticut regiment. In September 1775, the regiment joined Washington in Cambridge laying siege to the redcoat army in Boston. They entered the campaign that drove English troops from Boston the following March.

Washington then moved the bulk of his army toward New York. Hale marched with his regiment to New London, where they crossed Long Island Sound and headed for the city, which was occupied by the British army under Gen. William Howe. What Washington lacked was intelligence. After consultation with his staff, the general put out the word, seeking an officer who would undertake to go through the British lines into New York and return with reliable information. The 21-year old schoolteacher, now a Captain, was the only one to volunteer for the mission.

In early September, Nathan Hale traveled to Stamford, Connecticut. He crossed to Long Island in civilian dress, and carried his college diploma, to create a story as a visiting schoolteacher looking for work in the city. He made his way into Manhattan and spent a week moving around town collecting information. While Hale was attempting to return to Washington's camp, he was seized by a patrol from an English frigate. In the soles of his shoes his captors found the notes he had made, written in Latin. The papers clearly compromised him and he was returned to British-occupied Manhattan.

Hale was brought back into New York on September 21st, while the city was in the throes of a great fire. A quarter of the city burned. The British concluded, rightly or wrongly, that the fires had been set by the Americans and 200 people were jailed on suspicion of arson. It was not an auspicious moment to be dragged in front of General Howe. The papers found on his person were *prima facae* evidence of his intent. Hale acknowledged his name and rank. There was no trial; General Howe ordered his execution the next day. Early the next morning, Nathan Hale was led to his death. Hale asked for a Bible, but his request was refused. He was hanged at a spot near the present-day intersection of East Broadway and Market Streets. His final famous words were recorded by witnesses. "I only regret," Hale said, "that I have but one life to lose for my country." At 21, in our day, he would likely have been a junior in college.

Nathan Hale died as a partisan fighter and a partisan hero in America's War of Independence. Had Hale's cause been lost, though, and his footsteps to the gallows followed by John Adams, Thomas Jefferson and Nathaniel Greene, then his very existence would be a forgotten bit of colonial lore. Then again, of course, young Nathan Hale had no idea when he went to his death that he would be an honored hero to his country more than two centuries after his death.

His story reminds us at the very least that we can commit ourselves to a course of action, and even have the strength of character to live that commitment to its ultimate cost, but whether we become a heroic figure to others at least, generally lies outside our control. We can make choices that result in celebrated outcomes, but how those outcomes are celebrated are beyond our choosing.

CHAPTER 14

Jemima Nicholas: Local Hero, the Village Hero

There's nothing like a small-town hero. Cities, *big* cities and mega-cities have their own identities that often largely transcend the celebrity or accomplishments of individuals. Even heroes get lost in the kaleidoscope and wide-game of a New York, Houston or Los Angeles. Every village and small town out beyond the suburbs into rural America, though, celebrates its hometown heroes, someone who serves as a focal point for community pride, unique identity and local spirit. A local hero gives a community a claim to fame, a positive reason to put a place on the map.

Sometimes the local hero is someone born and raised in a locale, who then becomes famous on the broader stage of the outside world. Travel the stretch of old Route 66 that runs from Kansas to Tulsa and you soon drive through Commerce, Oklahoma. It doesn't take three blocks to discover that you're in the hometown of Mickey Mantle. A few miles down the road in Claremore is the homestead and museum devoted to Will Rogers. The Patsy Cline

Museum is in her birthplace of Winchester, Virginia. You don't have to spend long in Charlestown, New Hampshire to hear about local hero Carleton Fisk and over in Derry every schoolkid knows about native-son Alan Shepherd. Entertainer or athlete, politician, astronaut, or honored warrior: we love the story of small-town girl or boy who makes good.

Often, however, a local hero's fame remains far more localized, their feats of greatness performed on a smaller stage, their acts of courage or accomplishment of more immediate effect on their community. Up in Bamburgh, on the bleak northern English coast of Northumbria, a small museum commemorates Grace Darling, the lighthouse keeper's daughter, who accomplished a daring rescue pulling a longboat out to a floundering ship in a storm in 1838. The original boat is still there that she rowed through the North Sea. Grace Darling will long be the local hero of the Northumbrian coast.

I've always liked the story of Jemima Nicholas. She's a celebrated character out in Pembrokeshire, the southwest corner of Wales. Little is known about her life, but her extraordinary feat of chutzpah ought to give her a place in anyone's pantheon of heroes. Single-handedly, Jemima foiled the last land invasion of Great Britain and captured a Napoleonic army.

Invasions of Britain have been an intermittent occurrence since the time of Stonehenge. The Celts, the Romans, the Anglo-Saxons, the Vikings, the Normans: they have all had a turn. During the Battle of Britain, of course, Nazi bombers filled the skies of the island for months. The last *invasion* of Britain, however, took place on February 22, 1797. It was the time of the Napoleonic

Wars, and England and Wales anticipated that Napoleon might try to strike the southern coast.

It seems that a French fleet comprising some 1,400 Napoleonic troops were planning to attack Bristol or land in Ireland or some such (stories differ). They got blown off course, in any event, and landed in Fishguard Bay at the southwest tip of Wales.

The French warships off-loaded the troops and equipment on shore and promptly sailed away. It has never been clear exactly what their plan might have been; Fishguard is a long way from the back of nowhere. In any event, Napoleon was running amok on the Iberian peninsula and most everywhere else in Europe; the French emperor's first-rate troops were occupied elsewhere. The ragtag collection of soldiers and jailbirds that landed in Wales promptly neglected any military discipline and began a looting spree of the surrounding area—and sacked the pubs. A mounted messenger was hurriedly dispatched to summon the Pembrokeshire Yeomanry, the local militia, to come to the rescue.

Meanwhile, as the French soldiers were drinking themselves into bleariness, Jemima Nicholas, the wife of a Fishguard shoemaker, called all the local women and girls together surreptitiously and unfolded her audacious plan. She sent them all home to dress in their traditional Welsh costume of black skirts, red shawls and tall black felt hats and arm themselves with axes, pitchforks, hoes and other tools. Then, Jemima lined the women along the cliff tops surrounding Fishguard Bay. In silhouette against the fading light, the French thought the Welsh women were British soldiers.

When the local militia finally did arrive on the scene, the French troops, too drunk to fight, surrendered as prisoners of war. In the process, the feisty Jemima Nicholas herself, armed only with her pitchfork, single-handedly rounded up at least a dozen Napoleonic soldiers and put them in the Fishguard jail. One can only imagine that Jemima's shoemaker husband must have been a rather mild-mannered chap.

They have been telling the story in Pembrokeshire pubs for years. A memorial to Jemima Nicholas pays tribute in St. Mary's Church, Fishguard, where she is buried, and she has long been a heroine of local legend in southwest Wales. No documentary evidence of Jemima had been thought to survive. Recently, however, a local researcher doing work on his family genealogy uncovered Jemima Nicholas's 1755 baptismal record at the Pembrokeshire county records office in Haverfordwest.

Of all our representative heroes here, perhaps Jemima stands for the greatest number. These are the women and men unsung in the broader world, known only in their own localities or counties for the difference they made in the world—the lives they saved physically or metaphorically, the gifts they gave of self or substance, the acts of perseverance and courage that ennobled them and their communities.

Of course, one of the dangers of our society is our tendency to confuse heroism and celebrity. Being the birthplace of Billy the Kid, Al Capone or Benedict Arnold may make a place famous, but does not make heroism out of villainy. Notoriety and celebrity do not in themselves make an individual admirable, much less heroic. Genuine local heroes can provide an anodyne for the lessons of media and popular culture that project celebrity and fame as an end in themselves. Billy, Al and Benedict had to be born *someplace*, but all around us lie stories of self-sacrifice, devotion to a cause and personal nobility that serve as lessons for ourselves and the next generation.

Every town and city does not produce great sons and daughters like Babe Ruth, John Glenn and Jemima Nicholas, but every town has local heroes. Our old town histories in their annals tell countless stories of heroes lost in the footnotes and in the shadows, honored in the faded memories and legends of a community. Their exploits are perhaps honored with a monument, a monograph, a street name, a park, the naming of an elementary school or a town library. We ought to tell their stories over and over, to remind ourselves (and our schoolchildren) that heroes are real people and not distant media images.

CHAPTER 15

Titus Salt: Philanthropic Hero

I t is not likely there was any time in history when wealth was popular. The great majority of people, whether we call them working class, the masses or the poor have always been inclined to see wealth incorrectly as a zero-sum game. Yes, some people have egregious advantages and good fortune, and many people with wealth flaunt their narcissism and conspicuous consumption. The world has been like that since the days of the Egyptian pharaohs and is not likely to change soon. To help keep humankind from eating themselves alive over the unfairness of the world, God included a proviso in the Decalogue addressing the matter: Thou shalt not covet thy neighbor's ass or his other worldly accoutrements.

The excesses of superfluous wealth have been around for eons; so too, however, have the impulses to practical benevolence motivated by a love of humankind. From the beginnings of the industrial age, many magnates and superstars of the business world have given away huge portions of their amassed fortunes. Andrew Carnegie gave millions to fund libraries both in America and across Great Britain. Philanthropic foundations built on family fortunes such as Rockefeller Foundation, the Pew Charitable Trust, the Lilly Foundation, the Templeton Foundation and many others fund educational, cultural and humanitarian organizations and institutions. Bill Gates, Richard Branson and Warren Buffett are following in these footsteps. Private giving funds hospital wings and soup kitchens, medical research and symphony orchestras, college classrooms and disaster relief.

The greatest blessing of wealth isn't the accumulation of high-priced toys, it is the ability to give. When the gift of philanthropy enriches and nourishes the lives of many people, it is little wonder the memory of the giver is kept alive in the pantheon of heroes.

Through the late 18th and early 19th centuries, multitudes across the English midlands and North Country flocked from the land to the emerging factory towns burgeoning with the growth of manufacturing. Among the largest of these new industries was the production of textiles. In mills spread across Derbyshire, Cheshire, Lancashire and Yorkshire, factory chimneys sprouted like asparagus spears in a spring garden. In the Lancashire mill town of Bradford, for example, the population exploded from 13,000 to 104,000 in the first half of the 1800's, while more than 200 industrial chimneys spewed sulphurous, black fumes over the town. These were the "dark satanic mills" of William Blake's "Jerusalem."

Life was as nasty, brutish and short in the smoky, polluted mill towns as it had been in the 1200s. The Factory Act of 1819 set a working day for 9-year-olds of 12 hours, but it was sporadically and unevenly enforced.

From 1825, Saturday was a half day's holiday, with only nine hours of work; there were three full-day holidays a year.

The rapidly-growing towns were squalid and cramped, lacking basic sanitation or adequate water. Bradford earned a reputation as the most polluted town in England, but there were many candidates for the distinction. Raw sewage was dumped into the River Beck, the source also of the town's drinking water. Cholera and typhoid outbreaks were common. Life expectancy at birth was just over 18; half of all children died before their sixth birthday and only 30 percent lived to age 15.

Titus Salt was one of the few mill owners in his day to take concern for the welfare of his workers. Born in 1803, Titus Salt's father was a woolstapler, who started as a farmer and became one of the most successful wool merchants in Bradford. On his father's retirement in 1833, Salt took over the company and in the next 20 years became the largest employer in Bradford, and possibly the wealthiest. Salt's claim to fame was inventing a worsted cloth that combined alpaca with mohair, silk and coarser wools. His Alpaca Orleans was a cloth so fine that Queen Victoria kept two Alpaca herself at Windsor and sent their fleeces to have Salt turn them into cloth.

In 1842, Salt had found that a new device, the Rodda Smoke Burner, could largely eliminate the heavy polluting smoke and he had them installed at all five of his factories. When Salt was elected mayor of Bradford in 1848, he instituted a program to improve drainage and to provide for parks and other leisure facilities. Salt also urged the council to require all factories to use the new smoke burners. Other factory owners opposed the by-law and refused to accept that their factory smoke damaged the health of Bradford's citizens. Frustrated by the recalcitrance of the city council, in 1850 Salt announced that he would close his mills, leave Bradford and build a new factory community removed from the congestion and contagion of Bradford.

Three miles from Bradford on the banks of the River Aire Salt built Salts Mill. It was the largest and most modern textile factory in Europe. Over the next years, Salt built the surrounding village of Saltaire as home to his 3,500 workers. Along streets named for his children (and Queen Victoria), Salt built 850 homes for his workers, with gas mains and fresh water piped into each house. Beyond that, however, Salt built a hospital, a library, a Congregational church seating 600 people, public baths and wash houses, a school and institute, cricket pitches, parks and a boat house on the river—all out of his own purse. Saltaire was, he purposed, to be "a paradise on the sylvan banks of the River Aire, far from the stench and vice of the industrial city."

At the urging of local dignitaries, Salt stood for Parliament in the General Election of 1859 and won. After two years in the Commons, however, he resigned due to ill health. In 1869, Queen Victoria created Salt a baronet, making him Sir Titus Salt. The last building in Saltaire was completed in 1876 and Salt died just after Christmas a few months later.

Following his death, the *Bradford Observer* eulogized Salt: "Titus was perhaps the greatest captain of industry in England not only because he gathered thousands under him but also because, according to the light that was in him, he tried to care for all those thousands. . . . Upright in business, admirable in his private relations he came without seeking the honour to be admittedly the best representative of the employer class in this part of the country if not the whole kingdom." Mills for miles around closed as a mark of respect, while 120,000 people attended Sir Titus's funeral. While Salt had been an extremely wealthy man, his family discovered after his death that his fortune was no more. He had virtually given it away.

We admire easily enough those who work on the front lines to alleviate human suffering, whether it be in the Third World or in our own country. It is somehow emotionally more difficult to honor the philanthropy that funds such ends. Society envies extreme wealth and fawns over it, and, though we would all love to share such wealth, resents it.

It requires a real change of perspectives to admire the great good that is done by those who give their wealth away. While many people with fortunes become generous benefactors of society through a variety of causes, it is not that common to run across a man or woman who gives virtually all their wealth away. The example of Titus Salt, however, reminds us that there are many kinds of self-sacrifice.

CHAPTER 16

Mary Somerville: Hero of Science

"No circumstance in the natural world is more inexplicable than the diversity of form and color in the human race."

Let's see. We heat our water with microwaves, fly to the international space station, take antibiotics for a staph infection, toughen our teeth with fluoride toothpaste and ride to the office in a horseless carriage. Yes, we've come a long way from those pre-Enlightenment times when the general object of scientists was to convert base metals into gold.

There are so many heroes in the field of science. From the early days of folks like Francis Bacon and Isaac Newton to those women and men devoting themselves today to new discoveries in coronavirus and cancer research, our lives have been lengthened and bettered in innumerable ways by scientific advances made often with heroic effort. By applied study in the natural and physical sciences, many of the false notions that were not good for us and were not true have been laid to rest. Ironically, among the scientific discoveries upsetting the old perceived natural order is that women have an intellect capable of competing equally with men in the hard sciences. Tsk, tsk.

We hardly need to rehearse the educational disadvantages that women labored under in times past. It wasn't until the foundation of Somerville College in 1879, for instance, that women had any educational opportunity at Oxford University; it was not until 1920 that Somerville women were granted full University membership.

Over the years, the college was at the forefront of gaining full academic respect for women. Among its celebrated alumnae number Margaret Thatcher, Indira Gandhi, Dorothy Sayers and Nobel Prize chemist Dorothy Hodgkin. They all walked in footprints laid before them by the woman for whom their alma mater was named. Mary Somerville was the first British woman to gain an international reputation as a scientist and mathematician.

In a world where volumes of information on any subject imaginable, from origami to animism, is instantly accessible with a few clicks on the mouse, it is difficult to imagine how in the early 1800s Mary Fairfax Somerville taught herself as she did. Born in Jedburgh, Scotland in late 1780, Mary's father was a naval officer who rose to become a knighted vice admiral. Like the typical male of his day, however, he believed that education was not merely wasted on girls, but dangerous to their mind. She was taught to read, so she could read scripture, but it wasn't thought necessary that she learn to write. Her formal education consisted of a single year at a girl's boarding school near Edinburgh. Instead, she learned the accomplishments deemed appropriate for a young lady of her social class: piano, needlework and painting.

Mary Fairfax Somerville must be the quintessential autodidact. Despite being criticized rather than encouraged in her educational pursuits as a girl, she persevered, latching on to anyone who could advance her learning. When she visited an encouraging uncle in Jedburgh, the two would read Latin together before breakfast. With the help of her brother's tutor Mary studied Euclid's *Elements* and algebra. Her parents worried about her health because of the long hours of study she put in, often at night. In her memoirs, Mary recalls that when her father discovered her studying geometry, he cried to her mother, "Peg, we must put a stop to this, or we shall have Mary in a strait jacket one of these days."

A marriage in her 20s took Mary to London, but ended with the death of her husband after three years, leaving Mary two small sons. She returned to Edinburgh and found a circle of friends who encouraged her work in mathematics and science, including one John Playfair, professor of natural philosophy at Edinburgh University. He introduced her around and soon Mary was solving math problems with the best of the day. She also studied botany, geology, Greek and the principal texts of the day in math and astronomy.

Her second marriage was to her cousin, William Somerville, an inspector of hospitals. He was supportive of her study and took an active interest in science. When William was appointed Inspector to the Army Medical Board in 1816, the Somervilles moved to London—and moved in the leading scientific circles in the capital. Her study continued, and her life work began in earnest.

Somerville's reputation was secured with the publication of *The Mechanism of the Heavens* in 1831. Drawing upon the work of Frenchman Pierre LaPlace's *Mecanique Celeste* and expanding his work in differential calculus, Somerville produced the seminal English-language explication of the principles of astrophysics. Her *The Mechanism of the Heavens* was the field's primary text and first real textbook for two generations. Somerville reduces to mathematical equations the principles of universal gravitation, lunar theory and the movement of heavenly bodies in relation to each other and the Sun.

In 1832 Mary received notice that a marble bust of her was to be unveiled at the Royal Society for display in its great hall as an inspiration to its members. Here comes that irony again. They honored her with a bust, but denied her membership because she was a woman. Honors did pour in upon Somerville, however. She was elected to the Royal Astronomical Society and received honorary memberships in scientific societies across Europe and America. She even received a 200 pound a year pension from the Crown.

In subsequent books over the years, Mary Somerville predicted mathematically the existence of Neptune and Pluto and established timetables for such regular celestial events as the eclipses of Jupiter's moons. Her studies in the connection between the physical sciences anticipate by a century Einstein's search for a unified field theory. Her 1848 book, *Physical Geography* was a standard university text for half a century. Mary's last book, *Molecular and Microscopic Science*, was published in 1869, when she was 89.

It is hardly surprising that Mary Somerville became an outspoken supporter of women's education and women's suffrage. Not only did she teach herself and go on to be among the most significant physical scientists of the century, she did so during the intervals of raising five children and managing a Victorian household.

Mary Somerville died peacefully in Italy in 1872 at the age of 92. She was frail and deaf at the end of her life, but they say she spent four or five hours every morning reading books on higher math and solving problems. Obituaries in the London papers crowned her, and Mary Somerville has been since known as the Queen of 19th-century science.

When what became Somerville College was founded seven years later, Mary received perhaps the most appropriate honor of all. With her family's support, the Somerville family coat-of-arms became the crest of the college. It is impossible to know how many women, and men, have been influenced over the years by Mary Somerville's life and work. Though she always tended to deprecate her own contributions to science, the scientific community did recognize the value of her work. Like those of many of our heroes, Mary Somerville's story has faded into the dim and unrecognizable past; yet the tenacity and balance of her life provided a footprint in the sand with a lasting impact on our world.

CHAPTER 17

Huck Finn: A Literary Hero

"It is better to keep your mouth closed and let people think you are a fool than to open it and remove all doubt."

While there has never been official recognition given to a book as "the great American novel," certainly one of the prime candidates for such a title has long been Mark Twain's *Huckleberry Finn*. Writing through the latter decades of the 19th century, at his peak Twain was the most popular American celebrity of his time.

Born when Haley's comet was visible in the sky in 1835, Samuel Langhorne Clemens grew up in the Mississippi river town of Hannibal, Missouri. That was frontier life in the mid 1800s. Later, Twain would chronicle the town and its colorful inhabitants in his most famous works. Clemens always avowed that the name "Mark Twain" came from his years on the riverboat, where two fathoms (12 feet) or "safe water" measured on the sounding line was signaled by calling "mark twain."

As a humorist, satirist, short-story writer, lecturer and novelist, Twain was a prolific writer and public figure from the surprise popular success of the short story "The Celebrated Jumping Frog of Calaveras County" in 1867 until his death in 1910. *The Prince and the Pauper, Life on the Mississippi, The Adventures of Tom Sawyer* and *A Connecticut Yankee in King Arthur's Court* are among his most enduring works. Twain's greatest contribution to to American literature, however, is generally regarded to be *The Adventures of Huckleberry Finn.*

Literary folk have always been thrilled with *Huckleberry Finn* because it combines dramatic narrative, sparkling humor and social criticism in a unique way. Twain's talent for rendering the colloquial speech of 19th-century mid-America was a genuinely American literary voice and helped create and give identity to American literature. Both 20th-century literary greats William Faulkner and Ernest Hemingway found here in Twain the fountain and first fruits of American literature.

Today that same skilled use of local color has caused some folk to erroneously conclude a racist intent in the novel—condemning its accurate depiction of the language commonly used in 19th-century America. There are to this day occasional attempts to ban this great American masterpiece from public and school libraries. Yes, of course, expressions used unselfconsciously and casually then are today universally thought of as racist. That's the way it was. Apart from the general outrageousness of banning books in the name of political correctness, attempts to ban *Huckleberry Finn* in particular are ironically myopic. The moral stand taken by the great literary hero Huck Finn should not be lost on any of us.

While not exactly an orphan, Huck Finn is an essentially homeless boy left to bring himself up in the frontier river town of Hannibel. Rather like Robin Hood, Huck seems far more comfortable living with the natural law than he does with the strictures of society—in particular than with the strictures of a Hannibel, Missouri society presided over by the likes of Tom Sawyer's Aunt Polly and the Widow Douglas.

Huck Finn is, after all, largely a child of natural law. His lessons have been learned from a drunken, nomadic father, and from the civil and religious institutions on which he stands at the fringes. Huck lives a catch-as-catch-can existence with an easy-going attitude toward the world and a what-me-worry disposition. As Tennyson's Ulysses expresses it: "All experience is an arch where through gleams that untravelled world whose margin fades forever and forever as I move." Huck's escapades and adventures provide him with the education of experience and none of the baggage of society's pretenses and hyprocrises.

At the novel's climactic heart, Huck is sailing a raft south along the Mississippi River in the companionship of Jim, a good-hearted, gentle man who was, incidentally, a runaway slave. The Law is after them. More importantly, in Huck's mind, God is after them. Huck's formal religious education has been no more complete than his schooling. He has certainly, however, absorbed the normative religious lesson that the wages of sin are death, and that if he sins, God will send him to hell. In addition, Huck has absorbed the putative contention of his society that the chattel ownership of other human beings is the right, and that abetting a runaway slave is a *serious* sin.

Though Huck's two premises are flawed, our hero reasonably concludes that if he does not turn Jim in to the law, he will go to hell. This is not a comfortable position

for a boy to feel himself in; this is a moral choice none
of us would like to face. Many people today have a hard
time even imagining themselves in such an emotional and
intellectual situation. After all, you have to believe in God,
sin *and* hell to begin with. Beyond that, you have to believe
that what society generally believes and teaches trumps
natural law.

Such is Huck's crisis of conscience. Huck's conscience,
his gut instinct, *knows* that the right thing to do is to help
Jim to freedom, despite what the law (and assumedly, if
inaccurately, God's law) demands. Society has taught him
the wrong moral and theological lesson, but that does not
change the emotional trauma with which Huck wrestles.

"All right, I'll go to hell," Huck exclaims at the moment
of decision. He will remain loyal to his friendship with
Jim; he will recognize Jim's moral dignity and autonomy
as a man. Huck chooses to do what his conscience under
natural law knows to be the right, despite what he believes
to be the eternal severity of the consequence, and despite
the weight of social and religious opinion against his
choice. Ah, what a blow against political correctness.

Huck Finn comes down in history as a hero to all
those who long for the courage to be guided by conscience
and natural law instead of by a world of public opinion
and codified injustice. Huck's heroes might have been Don
Quixote and Robin Hood.

In the novel's famous final scene, Huck has returned
to Hannibal and the Widow Douglas has proposed to
adopt him. Huck is too much a free spirit, however, an
untamed innocent, to be tied down to the problems of
watching a clock, saying prayers, going to school, bathing
and keeping his elbows off the table. Huck purposes his

escape: "I've got to light out for the territory ahead of the rest," he proclaims. "They're going to civilize me," Huck grumbles, "and I don't like it; I've been there before." And so, Huck turns to the West, fulfilling America's Manifest Destiny, embodying the free spirit of the frontier. And who can blame him?

In 1909, Mark Twain predicted that as he had come in with Halley's Comet, he would go out with it. And so he did. The comet was visible in the sky when he died in April 1910.

CHAPTER 18

Edith Cavell: A Hero by Instinct

Often the actions of bravery and self-sacrifice that we regard as heroic are instinctive. A little boy falls off a darkened quay into the night ocean and an elderly woman standing nearby, with no thought for herself or her safety, plunges into the black water to rescue the tyke. Against all odds, she locates him in the churning waves; she manages to get the boy safely ashore and collapses herself dead on the strand. Yes, she is a hero. If the woman had taken the time to consider her action, however, it's likely that her better judgment would have prevailed (or been prevailed upon) and that she would not have jumped.

If the dear lady hero *had* paused to rationally consider the potential consequences of her plunge into the dangerous water, of course, it is likely that the delay would have cost the boy his life in any event. Her heroism and the life of the boy depended upon an action that was instinctive rather than deliberate. At the same time, if the brave woman had *lived* through the ordeal, her heroism would have been no less. The headlines in the local newspaper would just read very differently.

Whether she lived or died in the rescue of the lad, we know quite a lot about this anonymous lady from her reflex reaction on the harbor quay. Imagine an elderly woman who would do that. This was not someone who had frittered her years away. She took chances all her life, embarrassed her children, confronted perceived injustice, had opinions on life, was always physically active and enjoyed a sense of accomplishment. Right? The instinct that led her to the plunge in dark waters after the child was the expression of a character that was always there. That same instinct to heroic action, though, does not always show up as a reflex reaction; sometimes it simply marks almost matter-of-factly what must be done in the face of the danger.

When Edith Cavell was growing up at the vicarage in the Norfolk village of Swardeston, little could she have imagined that she was destined to become one of the most powerful symbols of English patriotism in World War I. Here, however, her upbringing and parentage developed in Edith both the personality and character such that when the moment came for a heroic decision, it was made by instinct rather than deliberative thought.

Both the vicarage where Edith Cavell spent her girlhood and the house in which she was born in 1865 still stand in the village some half a dozen miles southwest of Norwich. Her father held the living in Swardeston for 46 years. Edith was raised and educated in the customs of a late Victorian cleric's family, went off to Brussels as a governess, then trained in nursing at the London Hospital. She was a hospital nurse and by her evident dedication and leadership skills rose to become Matron. Fluent in French, in 1907 Cavell was put in charge of a pioneer nursing school in Brussels, providing nurses for several hospitals and several dozen schools.

When The Great War broke out, Cavell's clinic and school became a Red Cross hospital. After Brussels fell to the Germans, 60 English nurses were sent home, but Edith Cavell remained. As the German army advanced rapidly across Belgium, many retreating British and French soldiers were cut off behind German lines.

In the autumn of 1914, Cavell began sheltering stranded British soldiers, spiriting them out of the country to neutral Holland. Nurse Cavell's actions as a non-combatant behind enemy lines would be life-threatening under any wartime circumstances. As a medic under the protection of the Red Cross; she should have remained neutral.

Any crisis of conscience for Cavell, however, was swamped by her instinct to save the hunted men. A small underground cell developed with her leadership that allowed some 200 Allied solders to escape over the following months. All the while, she ran a Red Cross hospital caring for the wounded soldiers from both sides of the battle lines.

The next summer, a Belgian collaborator tipped the Germans of the clandestine operation. Along with several others of the escape team, Edith Cavell was rounded up and interned by the Germans. At her military trial, Cavell freely admitted that she "successfully conducted Allied soldiers to the enemy of the German people." Her fate was assured.

Cavell's death sentence by firing squad was carried out hurriedly and stealthily on October 12, 1915, despite the fervent intervention attempted by both United States and Spanish authorities. Cavell was hastily buried there at the rifle range where she was shot. Nurse Cavell became a martyr figure; military enlistment in Britain doubled in the eight weeks following news of her death. The huge international outcry following her execution swayed neutral opinion everywhere against Germany and eventually helped bring America into the war.

After the Armistice ending the war, Edith Cavell's body was returned to England. Crowds thronged the streets to pay tribute as her cortege passed through London. Following a service of memorial in Westminster Abbey, a special train conveyed her remains to Norwich. She was buried at a spot called Life's Green in the close of Norwich Cathedral where a fitting memorial marks her rest. A graveside service is held annually on the Saturday nearest the date of her death.

Across from London's National Portrait Gallery, where Charing Cross Road rises north out of Trafalgar Square, a statute of Edith Cavell remembers her. Its inscription echoes her words before facing the firing squad: "Standing as I do in view of God and eternity, I realize that patriotism is not enough. I must have no hatred or bitterness towards anyone."

Nature *and* nurture are both determinate factors in this kind of heroism. Nurse Cavell displayed a remarkable *sang froid* in her activities on behalf of trapped soldiers, in her demeanor during her trial and before the guns that would end her life. It was not adrenalin, glory or passion that motivated Cavell to courageous action. In her eyes, what she did was simply the natural extension of what she was. Cavell had the quiet capacity to subordinate her feelings—fear, hatred, self-righteousness, anger, self-preservation, vainglory—to do the right. That she had an unwavering understanding of what the right *was* she learned back in the vicarage in Swardeston.

Whether the example is jumping into black water at immediate personal jeopardy or living a clandestine life below the surface of everyday existence, there is a potential for heroism that is bred into us. How we were raised, how our children and grandchildren are brought up *does* make a difference in the kind of people we and they become. That's not an earth-shattering conclusion. Still, it seems one that is easily forgotten or often overlooked in practice these days. Stories like that of Edith Cavell give us needed reminders now and again.

CHAPTER 19

Helen Keller: Life Heroically Lived

"Character cannot be developed in ease and quiet. Only through experience of trial and suffering can the soul be strengthened, ambition inspired, and success achieved."

Life is tough enough to navigate with all five senses intact. Making do with less has always been a challenge in a world so apparently designed for all five. Being robbed of sight or hearing is regarded as the most debilitating of sensory handicaps. The loss of either faculty inevitably diminishes the quality of life and limits the range of human experience possible. It is difficult to imagine losing both senses and being lost in a silent, dark world that can only be navigated, communicated or understood by touch and scent.

Throughout much of history many kinds of disability brought a virtual exclusion from society in one way or another. Perhaps our world today is more aware of the difficulties imposed by any kind of physical handicap than ever before, and more sensitive to the needs and quality of life of those deprived of mobility or sensory experience. If that is so, a good deal of the credit goes to a woman who was both blind and deaf from infancy, but who grew up to become a role model for millions and who worked tirelessly for the betterment of others with disabilities.

Helen Keller was born, senses intact, in 1880 in Tuscumbia, rural northern Alabama. Her father planted cotton and edited a weekly paper. When Helen was 19 months old, she became seriously ill. Though her sickness was not diagnosed at the time, it is thought now to have been meningitis or scarlet fever. The toddler survived, but the fever left her without sight or hearing in a dark and silent world.

Those of us who have explored our world from cradle to adulthood with all five senses can have no conception of what it must be like to only know and recognize experience without hearing or sight, much less without either sense. The mind is intact, but receiving so much less sensory input than it is created for. It must have been intolerably frustrating for a bright little girl like Helen. As she grew, her bursts of temper and uncontrollability terrorized the Keller household. Today, we would say she was "acting out." Back then, family relatives thought she should be institutionalized, and her parents were desperate for some help.

Helen's mother sought the advice of a specialist in Baltimore, who sent her to see Alexander Graham Bell. Though Bell's fame rests on his invention of the telephone, much of his life's work was given to the education of the deaf. Bell, in turn, suggested they seek a teacher for Helen from Boston's Perkins Institution for the Blind. A visually impaired former student, young Anne Sullivan, was sent to become Helen's teacher.

Sullivan arrived in Tuscumbia in early 1887 and began to finger spell to Helen, but the girl had little understanding of what words meant. Anne moved herself and Helen out to a small cottage on the farm and began the arduous process of teaching Helen basic life tasks like fastening her shoes, brushing her hair and eating at table. After a month of frustration for both and limited communication between them, Helen's breakthrough moment arrived one day at the water pump. As the young teacher pumped water over Helen's open palm, she spelled the word over and over, and suddenly, as Helen described the moment years later, "the mystery of language was revealed to me."

From that beginning, Helen's progress was swift, as she showed an eagerness and a great capacity to learn. Anne Sullivan would stay with Helen as teacher and friend for almost 50 years—until her death in 1936. They moved together to the Perkins Institute in 1890, as Helen was more than ready for formal schooling. In 1900, Helen Keller entered Radcliffe; she graduated *cum laude* in 1904, the first deafblind person to earn a college degree.

After Keller's graduation, she began a career of writing and speaking. She wrote a dozen books, including *The Story of my Life* and *The World I Live In*, and scores of articles on women's rights and social issues as well deafness and blindness. Keller and Sullivan traveled the country on lecture tours. Despite Helen's deep desire to learn to speak, her speech never developed to the point of allowing her clear vocal communication. Sentence by sentence, Anne Sullivan would interpret Helen's thoughts and experience in front of rapt audiences.

Helen Keller's public espousal of socialism and her active support for the Socialist Party of Eugene Debs from 1909 to 1921 cost her some of her popularity with the public, but her enthusiasm for a public life remained undiminished. After Anne Sullivan's death, Polly Thompson became Helen's companion and interpreter. They traveled the world fundraising for the American Foundation for the Blind for 20 years. She also gave her support as well as her name to the Helen Keller Services for the Blind and the Helen Keller National Center for Deaf-Blind Youths and Adults.

The last decades of Helen Keller's life she lived at home in Westport, Connecticut. After she suffered a minor stroke in 1961, she retired from public life and died at 87 in 1968. Throughout a long, remarkable and productive life, Helen Keller met kings and presidents on every continent and was honored in many ways. She received the Presidential Medal of Freedom in 1964. She has been the subject of many books and films, most famously, 1962's *The Miracle Worker*, which garnered Academy Awards for Anne Bancroft and Patty Duke playing Anne and Helen. And Helen Keller is credited with introducing the Akita dog into this country and gaining its recognition as a breed.

As Keller became familiar with the world around her and with the range of human experience through the challenging years of her education, she would have become increasingly aware of the limitations of experience her disabilities imposed on her life. It would have been the path of least resistance to retreat into a sheltered and passive existence. Instead, Keller took the attack to life and devoted herself personally and professionally to enhancing the quality of life of those who shared in her blindness and her deafness.

The most striking element of Keller's remarkable life to me is that she spent it on the road. For half a century, her lifestyle and work was traveling: train stations and boats, airports and endless speaking venues, unfamiliar scents and cities, a faceless parade of anonymous hotel rooms. Traveling professionally always seems vaguely romantic to those who have never done it. Even those who love the lifestyle on the road, however, know its fatigues. Few people relish the experience as long as a dozen years. For Helen Keller to have kept her pace with the grace and enthusiasm she did for almost 50 years is nothing short of—heroic.

Indeed. Helen Keller's high-profile life and work did much to raise the public consciousness of such disabilities, to show the world that enormous contributions could be made by individuals despite their physical handicaps. She became a role model to countless thousands of youth and adults who have had to face the world with limitations on their sensory experience.

CHAPTER 20

C.S. Lewis: Cult Hero

*"You can't get a cup of tea big enough or a book long
enough to suit me."*

I t was Blaise Pascal who aphorized the truth we have
already noted that "the heart has reasons reason cannot
know." Regardless of our degree of erudition and self-
knowledge, every human being at times has both thought
and emotion that they find difficult to express, surmises
and feelings that never find their way into speech or
cogent thought. Then, we run across a novelist, a poet, a
songwriter, a thinker who shapes into words the intentions
of our heart and mind, who universalizes our experience
and confirms to us that we are not alone.

Emily Dickinson and Eminem, Bob Dylan and Rick
Warren, Jerry Garcia and Arthur Conan Doyle. Our cultural
history is full of figures who have become what we might
describe as cult heroes—attracting a huge following of folk
who identify with their themes and find in their lives and
craft a point of contact with something beyond themselves.

There are fan clubs and scholarly societies galore, people devoted to the appreciation and promotion of their iconic hero, be it Jane Austen or Bruce Springsteen. In its highest form, though, the cult hero rises beyond simply having an intellectual, artistic or emotional fan base to substantially influence our cultural history over several generations.

Consider C.S. Lewis. Perhaps no writer in history has been so deeply beloved by so many people for so many different reasons. In his superb medieval scholarship, his popular theology and apologetics, and his fiction, C.S. Lewis had an extraordinary gift for expressing thought just the way we wish we had thought it, and emotion just the way we feel it. Whatever topic he tackles, be it the human anguish of grief, the Elizabethan world view or the creation of Narnia, Lewis brings a crystal intellect and an imagination that universalizes our experience.

Lewis was being read and talked about on college campuses in the 1960s and remains so today. He is among the most influential writers in print. A quick Google search yielded 221,000,000 pages on Lewis—that would be 80 million more pages than Abraham Lincoln, with thrice the pages of Karl Marx or Charles Dickens.

Clive Staples Lewis was born in Northern Ireland in 1898. His middle-class parents had both Jack (as he was always known), and his brother, Warner, privately schooled in England. Lewis won a scholarship to University College, Oxford, but shortly after he arrived there in 1917, he enlisted in the army. He was commissioned an officer in the Somerset Light Infantry and landed on the front line in France on his 19th birthday.

After the war he returned to University College and took degrees in Greek and Latin, Philosophy and Ancient

History and English. In 1925 he was elected a Fellow of Magdalen College. Lewis was an Oxford don for almost 30 years, when he was elected to the Chair of Medieval and Renaissance Literature at Cambridge in 1954. He retained the seat until his retirement shortly before his death in 1963. John F. Kennedy and Aldous Huxley died on the same day.

Oxford's fall term of 1933 saw the founding of what became known as The Inklings. J.R.R. Tolkien, Owen Barfield, Neville Coghill and assorted other Oxford scholars and friends met Thursday evenings in Lewis's college rooms to read from their work in progress and talk. They met on Mondays or Thursdays around lunchtime at the Eagle & Child pub on Oxford's St. Giles (affectionately known as the "Bird & Baby"), to drink beer, smoke their pipes and set the world to rights.

Over the course of three decades, Lewis wrote more than 30 books. His major work as a literary critic includes *English Literature of the Sixteenth Century*, *The Allegory of Love*, and *The Discarded Image*. Lewis's widest popular audience has undoubtedly been generated by his fiction. The seven books of *The Chronicles of Narnia* are one of the most popular children's series ever—an amazing accomplishment for a middle-aged bachelor who had never been around children. It is, however, as a Christian thinker in a non-Christian-thinking world that Lewis rises above the level of mere scholar or popular author.

In such masterful works as *The Pilgrim's Regress*, *The Screwtape Letters*, *Mere Christianity*, *Miracles*, *The Great Divorce*, *The Problem of Pain* and more, Lewis does what Milton averred to do in the opening lines of *Paradise Lost*: justify the ways of God to men. Though Lewis was no formal theologian, he answers with clarity and coherence the ultimate questions of the world: If God is good, why is there evil in the world? What is the meaning and purpose of life? In the midst of His apparent silence, how do we comprehend God? In the body of his work, Lewis lays out a meaningful, articulate and comprehensive Christian world view that seems from his pen to be not simply reasonable, but obvious.

In a sense, Jack Lewis is the spiritual Odysseus and the Homer of our age. In his science fiction trilogy (*Out of the Silent Planet, Perelandra* and *That Hideous Strength*), his own thoughtful autobiography, *Surprised by Joy*, and his narrative nonfiction, Lewis is both the questing hero and the redactor of the quest. Now three generations of questing readers have found in Lewis the author who sparks the simple assent: "Of course." And Lewis's books become like the addictive peanut: you cannot read just one.

Perhaps C.S. Lewis becomes my example of the cult hero because as a writer he champions the heroic himself. The Pevensie children, Susan and Peter, Edmund and Lucy, all become heroes in Narnia and one by one exhibit the heroic in the choices of their lives. In *The Last Battle* gather around Aslan the heroes of Narnian history, like Reepicheep, Tumnus and the Beavers, in a roll call of honor. Throughout the Space Trilogy there are clear and clear-eyed heroes from Ransom to Merlin, rising from suspended animation in the center of the earth.

Lewis's elevation of the hero and heroic virtue in his fiction is inspiring and uplifting. Few readers from childhood to the wisdom-of-the-ages can fail to want to identify their lives with the convictions and character of Lewis's leading men and women, boys and girls.

Beyond his fiction, however, and throughout the canon of his books, Lewis assembles for his readers an inventory of struggles and characteristics in human life that would be heroic. The Lewis hero is someone who experiences pain and endures it with grace and understanding, who believes against all natural odds in miracles, who undergoes grief and comes to peace, who wrestles with the hard questions of human existence and finds answers, who quests with purpose and with meaning, who is surprised by joy, who loves with knowledge and abandon, who discovers God for themselves.

Intellectual fashions, literary fashions and spiritual fashions come and go through the generations. Some rare few thinkers and writers, though, speak to the human spirit with such a clear, true voice that they transcend those styles and tastes of culture—Shakespeare and Dante, Milton and Augustine—and C.S. Lewis. Only history will tell for sure, of course, but Lewis is one for the ages. Rock on, Jack!

CHAPTER 21

Ronald Reagan: The Political Hero

"Freedom is never more than one generation away from extinction. We didn't pass it on to our children in the bloodstream. It must be fought for, protected, and handed on for them to do the same."

Historians will forever debate the merits and limitations of Ronald Reagan as a president. Then again, they do that with every president. Perhaps not enough time has gone by to give the perspective to the Reagan presidency that it will have in another generation or three. Time tends to blur the politically partisan perception that we have toward presidents of our own ken. There seems no question, however, that Franklin Roosevelt and Ronald Reagan are the most historically significant presidents of living memory. Whether or not you sympathize with one or the other, clearly each of them is a hero in their own way, and to millions of people.

Apart from what they accomplished that made them heroes, Ronald Reagan certainly had the more heroic persona. Whether or not that translates into a larger historical profile than Roosevelt's in future centuries remains to be seen. It probably will. After all, Roosevelt came from a silver spoon background, and while he modeled exceptional courage in governing through his debilitating paralysis, neither of those characteristics are propitiously heroic.

Before Reagan became a political figure in any sense, he had already created a heroic persona for himself and in the eyes of the public. It's all well and good to dismiss Reagan's acting career by describing him as a B-list actor. In reality, through the '40s and early 1950s, Reagan was a well-known screen star with rugged good looks and more than his share of heroic roles.

Yes, it is *Bedtime for Bonzo* that seems to be the role he has been known for early in the 21st century. In 1944, however, American patriotic fervor was righteous and all-encompassing in daily life, as American GI's were dying in the Pacific at a greater rate per day than have lost their lives in any conflict since. Ronald Reagan took top billing in MGM's Irving Berlin musical tribute to the fighting man *This Is the Army*. It was an all-star cast that included Berlin himself singing "This Is the Army" and Rosemary DeCamp, George Murphy, Alan Hale and Una Merkel. It was Kate Smith's film debut singing "God Bless America," introducing the song into our culture. Ronald Reagan played the lead and the love interest—the soldier who ends up with the girl.

As a platform from which to launch a political career . . . Arnold Schwarzenager eat your heart out. Interestingly enough, George Murphy too went on to a political career and became Senator from California. Reagan already had an actor's heroic public persona, certainly in California, by the time he became president of the Screen Actors Guild in 1954. He moved on to the national stage in the 1960s, became governor of California in the 1970s and subsequently, of course, President.

In his 1980 campaign, there was a defining moment that gave him a real life heroic dimension. It seems a minor incident in the reading. As political historians attest, however, the event may have made his candidacy. During the New Hampshire Primary, a public forum was held in Nashua, sponsored by the Reagan campaign and moderated by local media. When a slightly officious moderator attempted to prohibit George H.W. Bush, then one of Reagan's primary opponents, from participating, Reagan took great umbrage and with authority declared: "I'm paying for this microphone."

The tone and timbre of Reagan's voice were virtually the same when, seven years later, Reagan stood squarely on the world stage before Berlin's Brandenburg Gate on July 12, 1987 as Eastern Europe teetered and challenged: "Mr. Gorbachov, tear down this wall."

Remember Churchill's whimsical assessment of his own celebrated role in World War II: "It was the nation and the race dwelling all round the globe that had the lion's heart. I had the luck to be called upon to give the roar." Certainly, the economic and ideological underpinnings of Communism were largely a spent force by the 1980s. That the Iron Curtain, and the Berlin Wall, came tumbling down can hardly be attributed solely to Reagan's White House leadership. Nonetheless, he was the world leader most individually responsible; at the very least, in Churchillian terms, Reagan gave the roar.

Any poll of Americans these days puts Abraham Lincoln at or near the top of charts for presidential greatness. Lincoln had his own roar, and his own defining moments. The Emancipation Proclamation, the Gettysburg Address and his tragic end as the first American president to be assassinated in office are elements of Lincoln's history that every American ought to be able to recall. After a century and a half, however, apart from Lincoln's prosecution of the Civil War and his determination to preserve the Union, few people could recall a single detail of his domestic policies, the quality of his judicial appointments or even his general philosophy of government.

It does not matter. When a person's character, place in time and events align to elevate them to the iconic status of a hero, other attributes and elements of their life history become largely irrelevant. Like Churchill and Reagan, Lincoln gave the roar. Of course, there is a lot more to Lincoln and Churchill as men and as national leaders, as those who study history and politics will bear witness. But it was the roar that makes them timeless heroes.

Just so, as two generations pass, Ronald Reagan will be remembered as one of history's heroes, among the greatest world leaders of all time. In the highly charged atmosphere of the political present, that is a controversial assertion. Reagan fans will be nodding their heads in assent at my judgment. Just as many non-Reagan admirers will be ready to toss the book aside in disgust, concluding me to be thoroughly discredited thereby. It was the lion's roar.

Reagan's judicial philosophy, economic policy and social politics will blend into the landscape of 20th-century

American political history—evaluated in broader contexts than our experience or our times. A century from now, historians alone will be remembering the Bork nomination, the cultural squabbles of the 1980s or Reagan's role in the economy of the decade.

'Twas the stuffed 19th-century political philosopher Jeremy Bentham who articulated the Utilitarian maxim of evaluating government: that policy is good that provides the greatest good for the greatest number. An apropos variation on that theme might evaluate political leaders historically by their contribution to ameliorating the human condition. Ronald Reagan stood on the point and roared as the Iron Curtain came down, the Soviet Empire unraveled and a score of countries left the economic and human rights misery of communism for emerging democracies.

As the roar, Reagan won the Cold War. Without firing a weapon. Never in world history have as many people's lives been so beneficially affected at a single stroke by a political victory. If the world continues to avoid nuclear winter and solar summer for another three centuries, the few paragraphs in high school World History that cover the second half of the 20th century will recall Reagan as the political hero of his generation.

CHAPTER 22

Stan Rogers: The Hero Gone Too Soon

"Ah, for just one time I would take the Northwest Passage
To find the hand of Franklin reaching for the
Beaufort Sea;
Tracing one warm line through a land so wild and
savage
And make a Northwest Passage to the sea."

Northwest Passage

I t is almost painful to speculate what our world would
be had not so much genius, leadership, creativity and
heroism been lost that could have come from those
promising individuals throughout history who died before
fulfilling their potential contributions to the world.

What music will we never hear because Mozart died
at 34? What unwritten poetry died with John Keats at
21? How much promise was lost on both sides in the
lives of millions who died across the trenches of World
War I? Where would the Camelot of John F. Kennedy's

administration have brought us had he not been gunned
down in Dallas in 1963?

I went to a ceilidh in Port Hawkesbury some 20 years
ago, where Cape Breton greets the northeastern Nova
Scotia coast across the Strait of Canso. It was there I met
the music of Stan Rogers. This ceildih was not a seasonal
production for tourists, but a community gathering, several
hundred local folk and summer visitors, in the old train
station. Home baked goods and coffee were sold in the
back of the hall. A young step dancer was put on first in the
program so he could get home early; he'd be milking cows
at five a.m. The fiddlers, dancers and singers from that
part of Nova Scotia had a great evening, with a rollicking
audience that was often invited to join the music.

The greatest applause of the evening erupted when
the young compere announced that he was going to do a
song by the late Stan Rogers. He sang at the piano "Tiny
Fish for Japan." Many in the audience were moved to
tears. It was not until years later I learned that Rogers
was writing about the freshwater fisheries of Lake Erie.
So universal to the Canadian experience is Rogers' music.

At its simplest, Stan Rogers was a singer/songwriter.
While he is largely an unknown to most of the world, his
many fans proclaim that he was the greatest ever Canadian
folksinger. Perhaps he was. Born in Hamilton, Ontario in
November 1949, Stan Rogers grew up in the rural Great Lakes
Region. He played acoustic guitar (and some rock bass). Stan's
hero was Gordon Lightfoot, and he gravitated into the rich
Canadian folk music scene in the late 1960s and early 1970s.

Though he was brought up in Ontario, Stan's parents
were Maritime people and Stan spent summers in Nova
Scotia with family. Up in the Maritimes, on Nova Scotia's

Cape Breton Island especially, they have an indigenous Celtic music brought over from Scotland 300 years ago. In fact, some musicologists opine that Cape Breton music is the purest existing Celtic music—less tinged by the musical influences of other traditions. Still, Stan Rogers songs flowed easily into the musical traditions of the Atlantic Provinces when he celebrated their world in his debut album *Fogarty's Cove* in 1976.

Nova Scotia, Prince Edward Island, Newfoundland and New Brunswick: they farm in the Atlantic Provinces; there's timber and some mining; but they've always lived from the sea. The coast of Atlantic Canada lies pocked with harbors and fishing villages. Out on the cold North Atlantic, they plied the water for generations in George's Banks and beyond, pulling haddock and cod from the dark waters. Then more than a generation ago now, along came the fish factories from the Soviet Union and Japan, huge ships that were self-contained processing plants, that vacuumed the Banks of everything swimming. And the cod became fished thin, and a way of life began to die. Rogers captured the soul and quiet dignity of the hurting fishing villages and grim mining towns in songs such as "Fogarty's Cove" and "Make and Break Harbor":

> *"In Make and Break Harbor the boats are so few*
> *Too many are pulled up and rotten.*
> *Most houses stand empty, old nets hung to dry*
> *Are blown away, lost and forgotten."*

Sometime after the strong success of *Fogarty's Cove*, Rogers conceived the idea of an epic cycle of Canadian albums. He was writing and singing about the experience and identity of being Canadian. Like many Canadians, Rogers was quite aware of being overshadowed in popular culture and history by America: "I've had the motive of trying to make my countrymen a bit more aware of just how fascinating their own history is."

Next, he turned to the Canadian Prairies and the West with an album titled *Northwest Passage* released in 1981. It was intended as the second in a five-album Canadian suite. The title song speaks of following in the footsteps of early Canadian explorers like Simon Fraser, John Franklin and David Thompson.

"I've always made kind of a great deal of what Canadian heroes we had and there were plenty of them," he said. He pointedly sought to dramatize the events of Canadian history and inject them into the popular culture with his music.

By the early 1980s, Rogers was in demand on the folk circuit both in Canada and America, winning acclaim for the unique voice his music gave to the Canadian experience and the lives of those who worked the farms, the mines and the fisheries. He took on a grueling performance schedule. Bearded and balding, Rogers was a big man—6'4" and thick-framed. He sang with a broad-ranging baritone voice, full of resonance and emotion.

At the same time, Rogers began a two-year project to write and create the third album of the series, turning to his home region of the Great Lakes. Port Dover on Lake Erie, once home of the largest freshwater fishing fleet in the world, shares an eerily similar fate to that of Make and Break Harbor. Stan tells the story in the haunting "Tiny Fish for Japan." The album, *From Fresh Water*, was released posthumously.

Stan Rogers died in an airplane fire at the Cincinnati airport in June 1983. He returned into a burning plane to help rescue those trapped—and never made it out. He was 33. Stan and his music belongs to all of Canada, but he is thought of first with the Maritime Provinces and especially loved in Nova Scotia. Up in Canso Town, on Nova Scotia's northeast coast across the Strait of Canso from Cape Breton, the Stan Rogers Folk Festival every summer brings together a generation of musicians and fans influenced by his brief career and music.

Like Homer's Odysseus journeying home to Ithaca, Stan Rogers crossed Canada on the quest, and wrote of questing heroes. His metaphor was the legendary Northwest Passage:

> *"How then am I so different from the first men*
> *through this way?*
> *Like them, I left a settled life, I threw it all away*
> *To seek a Northwest Passage at the call of many men*
> *To find there but the road back home again."*

The music of Stan's songs is as simply elegant and memorable as his lyrics. He wrote of Canada's questing heroes, both famous and historic, unheralded and quiet. He championed Canada's unique identity and the experience of Canadian life. His surviving discography consists of six total albums, including two live performances. Folks up in Canso will tell you Stan Rogers was a hero gone too soon.

If a single song captures the lyric legacy of Stan Rogers, however, it must be *"The Mary Ellen Carter."* The eponymous lady was a sunken fishing boat in the cold North Atlantic water raised by the grit and determination of the men who loved her. The song has been called an anthem, and is often thought of as the song by which Stan's friends and admirers remember him:

> *"And you, to whom adversity has dealt the final blow*
> *With smiling bastards lying to you everywhere you go*
> *Turn to, and put out all your strength of arm and heart and brain*
> *And like the Mary Ellen Carter, rise again.*
> *Rise again, rise again—though your heart it be broken*
> *And life about to end.*
> *No matter what you've lost, be it a home, a love, a friend.*
> *Like the **Mary Ellen Carter**, rise again."*

CHAPTER 23

The Plague Village of Eyam: Collective Courage and Heroism

Heroism is an individual thing. We can't be a hero for someone else, nor can we ride to honor and glory on the coattails of another. If heroism can not be a collective attribute, however, there are times when a heroic result can only be achieved by the concerted action of more than one individual's decision and effort.

Being a firefighter is a tough job; the heroic actions of many NYFD personnel in the immediate aftermath of the 9/11 devastation at the World Trade Center dramatically reminded the world that firefighting is not only one of the most physically dangerous occupations, but also one most susceptible to putting its men and women in situations calling forth actions of heroic character. Newspaper archives from Jacksonville to Eugene reveal stories of firemen risking their own lives and limbs to secure the safety of those trapped and threatened by the flames. Heroes all.

Sometimes, it might be that the successful rescue of the dear old woman or the bubbly bouncing baby girl requires the life-threatening commitment of *two* firefighters. Two individuals have to have the motivation, will and courage to enter the burning and collapsing building in order to successfully effect a rescue. If only one firefighter makes that decision and commits to the action, there is no heroic outcome—the bird or baby dies in the flames. That unfortunate outcome is the same, of course, if two heroic firefighters enter the burning building on the rescue mission and die themselves in the attempt.

If the happy, hopeful mission is accomplished because two firefighters each had "the right stuff"—damsel in distress is successfully saved from the conflagration—then there are two heroes. Though their action was concerted, the heroism was individual, not collective. Imagine, if you will, a concerted action of heroism that depended not upon two individuals of self-sacrificing determination, but upon 350.

In June 1665 the Bubonic Plague struck London. The great Samuel Pepys recorded in his diary: "This day much against my will, I did in Drury Lane see two or three doors marked with a red cross upon the doors and 'Lord have mercy upon us' writ there—which was a sad sight to me, being the first of that kind that to my remembrance I ever saw." In the weeks to come, one in four Londoners died, and the plague spread throughout England.

In the village of Eyam, high in the Derbyshire Peaks of the English midlands, one George Vicars, a tailor, took delivery of some cloth from London in August. On September 7th, Vicars died of the lethal bacteria carried in the cloth. Though the plague had arrived in Eyam, however, the surrounding villages and the countryside were yet free of the deadly pestilence.

The parish vicar, Rev. William Mompesson, proposed that to prevent an epidemic the villagers voluntarily quarantine themselves, isolating the village from the world outside and confining the spread of the deadly disease. No one would leave Eyam, and no one would be allowed to enter the village. Mompesson urged upon the villagers their remembrance of John 15:13: "Greater love hath no man than this, that a man lay down his life for his friends."

With the knowledge of almost certain death and aware of the sacrifice they were making, Eyam's villagers agreed to stay. They created a cordon around the village, cutting themselves and the disease off from the world. As the months went by, the death toll from bubonic plague in Eyam grew. Scarcely a household remained unaffected as one by one whole families succumbed to the plague bacteria *Yersinia pestis*.

For more than a year, the village of Eyam held firm to its quarantine as its population inexorably dwindled. Church services were held in the open air so that the worshippers could stand apart from each other—"social distancing." Neighboring villagers brought food, supplies and news of the larger world to the edge of town. Conversations were shouted across the fields and the people of Eyam knew that their quarantine was effective; the plague had not spread to other villages. In August 1666, Rev. Mompesson lost his own wife, Katherine, to the rapacious disease.

And then the plague ran its course. On November 1, 1666, Abraham Morten became the last victim of the plague in Eyam (and the 18th member of his family to die). Some 90 survivors were left from a village population of 350. Around the village, 260 people had been buried in hastily dug pits on the land their ancestors had worked for centuries. The act of self-quarantine and self-sacrifice of the villagers of Eyam, however, was successful in saving thousands of lives and countless suffering across the county of Derbyshire and the surrounding region.

The people of Eyam, living and dead, were heroes. Their heroism was individual, however, not collective. The decision of each villager was a personal and voluntary action. There is no indication in the well-documented annals of Eyam's story that there was any coercion or recalcitrance in the decision of the villagers to act as they did. Their society did not exist as an entity apart from the sum of its individuals. Yet their individual heroism undertaken merely as individuals would have had little impact on the advance of the plague through the Peak District. Moreover, however heroic the action of a single individual, it would have been swallowed unnoticed by history. By acting together, the noble citizens of Eyam were able to affect a heroic action remembered in history that was much greater than the sum of their own lives and actions could have ever been.

The story of Eyam has an unusual postscript. Because there were clear village records of victims and survivors of the Eyam siege, family lines of the plague survivors exist today and have been traced. Medical researchers at University College, London have detected in direct descendents of Eyam survivors the presence of a mutated "survival gene." The bubonic plague commandeers the white blood cells sent to attack the bacteria and uses them to enter the lymph nodes, except when blocked by this genetic mutation—CCR5 delta 32. Pharmaceutical companies used the information to develop early inhibitors—drugs that mimic the effects of CCR5 mutations and help block a modern plague that attacks the immune system—HIV.

In looking at some of the heroes we have been considering, we may indeed examine ourselves and seek to encourage in ourselves the attributes of character that are heroic. Even if those character traits are in us, however, it may require both the circumstances and heroic character of others to find its expression.

Another lesson from Eyam is more humbling. Like angels unawares, there may be peopling our everyday lives many individuals whose own lives are lived in heroic action and with heroic character completely outside our awareness of it. They live it quietly and daily and nothing extraordinary about their daily life would betray it to the world.

CHAPTER 25

Harriet Tubman: Underground Hero and "Moses of her People"

"There is one of two things I had a right to—
liberty or death."

In the early 21st century, no less than in the past, we live in a dangerous and often cruel world. There is no end of misery around the globe: coronavirus, malnutrition, HIV, incomprehensible living conditions and the deep social wounds made by civil wars and natural disasters are constants. Thanks to the modern miracles of instant global media and communication, we have unprecedented awareness of the suffering in African civil wars, the human toll of California wildfires, the dislocation and destruction caused by Atlantic hurricanes and sundry natural and human produced disasters.

America *is* responsive to these acute needs as a nation. We are the most generous people on earth, both in our personal giving and in our national response to the traumas of the human condition. Still, while we know this human suffering is going on, blessedly, "out of sight, out of mind" is also a natural characteristic of human consciousness. Unless it is touching someone about whom we care personally, or in some way impacting our own lives, most of us are not hard-wired to feel the pain of others.

What motivates one individual rather than another, rather than you and me, to feel personally motivated to risk their own lives in order to rescue others from any variety of human suffering, remains a mystery.

Born into slavery on Maryland's eastern shore around 1820, Harriet Tubman began work as a house servant at age five or six. At about 12, she was assigned to field work. In her early teens, Harriet was struck in the head by a two-pound weight thrown by an angry overseer. She never completely recovered from the injury and suffered from narcolepsy throughout her life.

In 1849 Harriet Tubman feared she and other plantation slaves were to be sold South. Harriet ran. A white neighbor set her on the Underground Railroad to freedom. Traveling by night and following the North Star, she made her way to Pennsylvania.

"I has reasoned this out in my mind," she said, "there is one of two things I had a right to—liberty or death."

In Philadelphia, Tubman found work and met William Still, Philadelphia Stationmaster on the Underground Railroad. Through Still and others in the Philadelphia Anti-Slavery Society, Tubman joined the UGRR. She returned to Maryland to begin the rescue of her family in 1851, relocating them to St. Catherine's, Ontario, which she made her base of operation: first, her sister and her sister's children, then her brother and two other men, and finally her 70-year old parents.

Again and again she returned to the South finding other fleeing slaves to escort north to freedom. Tubman became the most famous conductor on the Underground Railroad. Slaveholders and slave hunters actively sought her capture. In 1856 the posted bounty on her head in the South was $40,000. Yet Tubman was undeterred and seemingly oblivious to any concern for her own life or safety.

Tubman would disappear for weeks at a time and make detailed preparations for each flight to the North. Like any successful undercover agent, she developed elaborate ruses and strategies to lead scared fugitive slaves across actively hostile country and on north to Canada and their liberty.

One key to Tubman's success on her extraordinary missions was her very plain, unassuming appearance. By all accounts, however, Tubman was a pretty tough character. She carried a revolver with her, not to defend herself against those who sought her life, but with which to threaten those of her passengers who tired of the rigors of the journey or wanted to turn back. As she claimed later with some justifiable pride, "I never lost a single passenger."

When she was not on the road, Tubman took a vocal part in antislavery meetings and raised funds to support her work and the Underground Railroad. She became friends with leading abolitionists such as Frederick Douglas and John Brown. By 1860, Harriet Tubman had made the life-hazarding journey South 19 times. It is reckoned she conducted more than 300 runaway slaves to safety and freedom in the North.

During the Civil War, Tubman worked for the Union, serving variously as a cook, a hospital nurse, a scout and a spy. From the late 1850s, Harriet Tubman's base of operations (and where she relocated her family) had been Auburn, New York. The town on the Underground Railroad was home to many sympathetic Quakers and abolitionists. U.S. Senator and former New York Governor Charles Seward and his wife provided her a home there. After the war, she returned to Auburn and in 1869 she married Nelson Davis, a soldier she had met in 1863 while she was leading black Union soldiers on raids along South Carolina's Comcahee River.

After Davis's death in 1888, Tubman purchased a 25-acre parcel of land, which she later deeded to the AME Zion church. The Harriet Tubman Home was opened in 1908 where from 12 to 15 aged and indigent African Americans were given a home. Tubman died there in her early 90s in 1913. Though the home continued to operate after her death, it was finally closed and the building vacated in 1928. The Harriet Tubman Home was restored by the AME Zion church in 1953 as a memorial to the life and work of this remarkable woman. Today, the complex at the Harriet Tubman Home not only includes the original frame building, but an assembly hall and library, and is regularly used for educational programming and youth conferences.

Harriet Tubman became lauded in her lifetime as the "Moses of Her People." She rather puts me in mind of Shakespeare's Miranda, described in *The Tempest*: "Though she be but little, she is fierce." It is so easy to simply recount the exploits of Harriet Tubman, but difficult indeed to walk in her moccasins: a young illiterate black woman going time and again behind enemy lines, daily placing herself in the hands of people who at any time could betray her for profit or take her life with impunity.

Where does it come from, that spark that ignites the soul with such a selfless passion? Like the crimes of a convicted cat burglar or embezzler, again, a heroic action requires the same components of opportunity, means and motive. Opportunity abounds; as we have remembered, our globe contains no end of disease, ignorance and ignominious poverty to be ameliorated. And there are new and immediate causes that arise in the world every week.

As to motive . . . . In truth, much as we rightly admire their selflessness and sacrifice, most of us do not aspire to the spark that motivated people like Harriet Tubman, Mary Slessor and Dietrich Bonhoeffer. Mustering a small cup of the milk of human kindness from time to time is about the best we can handle on a regular basis. It is the extraordinariness of that motivating spark that makes them heroes.

Oh, and as for *means*, as Harriet Tubman bears witness: where there's a will, there's a way.

CHAPTER 26

William Booth: Hero with a Cause

"Go straight for souls, and go for the worst."

I f the exploits of Don Quixote seem to be those of a crusader without a cause, history is replete with those who might have been inspired by his idealism and his sheer fearless dedication. Those who end up in our pantheon of heroes, though, gave their devotion and their lives to causes as unique as themselves—St. Francis of Assisi, Clara Barton, Martin Luther King, Albert Schweitzer, Susan B. Anthony, William Wilberforce.

Our world today is full of *unsung* heroes who are utterly dedicated to causes for which they give their lives. They are running soup kitchens and homeless shelters, teaching Bible classes, sheltering animals, counseling abuse victims, visiting nursing homes, operating medical stations in Africa and crusading for human rights around the globe. The difference between unsung heroes and those whose name we know is often found in the continuing legacy of an organization or institution that some heroes leave behind whether they set out to do so or not. In fact, sometimes the legacy goes on to eclipse its founder entirely.

William Booth was born in Nottingham in 1829. Following the death of his father, Booth was apprenticed at age 13 to a local pawnbroker. While still a teenager, Booth came under the teaching of fiery itinerant Methodist preachers and became convinced that God was calling him to spread the Gospel. He moved to London, as both a preacher and pawnbroker. In 1855, he married Catherine Mumford and spent the next few years as a Methodist New Connection minister posted on a preaching circuit.

Booth developed a flamboyant fire-and-brimstone preaching style and used hymns sung to popular musical hall tunes of the day. Though his style and message attracted the working poor of Victorian England, Booth's methodology if not his message stirred up criticism among the staid clergy of the Establishment.

After preaching a series of meetings in London's grim and seedy East End, Booth was so moved by the needs of East London's urban poor that he and Catherine left the road to establish The Christian Mission in East London. Reasoning fairly enough that people with empty stomachs are not going to be attentive to their souls, the Booths tackled the huge social needs of the East End as well as proclaimed God's Word, opening soup kitchens and "Food for the Millions" shops to help feed London's starving poor.

What began as a mission became a movement that addressed human need both physical and spiritual. While William preached in pubs, stables and the open air, Catherine raised funds. Booth's mission and fame kept growing as his ministry struck a chord with those whose social needs he addressed and those who felt displaced from the "respectability" of traditional churches.

In 1878, Booth's organization became the Salvation Army. It adopted the military organizational structure and terminology that are recognizable today. With its newspaper called *The War Cry*, brass bands and the motto "Blood and Fire," the Salvation Army rallied people to their cause. Though Booth never intended to begin a church, by 1885 there were 910 corps (churches) and 2,300 officers in Britain. By then, there were Salvation Army corps as well in the U.S., France, Australia and India. In addition to spreading the word of God, under the leadership of both Booths, the Salvation Army crusaded against prostitution, alcohol and social injustice; it crusaded for homeless shelters, lost person bureaus and prison reform.

Through every aspect of the Salvation Army, Catherine Booth worked beside her husband as an equal in ministry, in preaching as well as organization. In fact, the Salvation Army was the first church or parachurch organization to recognize women as equals in ministry and leadership.

In the later years of his life, General William Booth became an itinerant preacher again, criss-crossing the world with the message of the Salvation Army. Through his 70s he made annual tours of Britain, speaking at hundreds of meetings and traveling thousands of miles in failing health. Booth died in 1912 at age 83. Some 150,000 people waited in line to pass his funeral bier in tribute. In Salvation Army terms, General Booth had been Promoted to Glory.

Today, the Salvation Army is commonly regarded as one of the most effective, efficient charities in the world.

In addition to its nationwide program of first-response disaster relief, Salvation Army programming directly aids some 34 million people in almost 9,000 communities across the United States. Its international headquarters in London coordinates the work of national Salvation Army corps in 106 countries. True to its origins as a band of people committed both to proclaiming the love of God and serving the disadvantaged of society, the Salvation Army is a stellar example of faith-based social services— and the legacy of an unlettered apprentice pawnbroker from working class Nottingham.

Few of us combine the evangelistic fervor, front-of-the-house personality, social imperviousness and ability to inspire action in others shared by the founding leaders of so many causes. What route they took themselves to become leaders of movements or organizations, neither Booth nor Elizabeth Cady Stanton, Lord Baden Powell or Billy Graham knew the destination they would reach at the start of the journey. At some point, however, they each began with the decision or discovery: "I can do some good with my life." Then, they acted on it. They were activists long before anyone ever heard of them, let alone before they were "heroes."

There is an old saying which reminds us that every journey begins with a single footstep. It may not seem that warrior heroes like Odysseus, Charlemagne or Lord Nelson have much in common with William Booth— despite the military trappings of the Salvationists and the General's respected rank. But they took that decisive footstep; they were people of action. Don Quixote, David Livingstone, Harriet Tubman and Ernest Shackleton could have all stayed home. The one characteristic of all heroes is that they are people of action.

Regardless of our personalities, our physical and intellectual abilities, or our particular talents or lack thereof, every individual can be an activist. It may be difficult or impossible for us to personally identify with the disparate heroes we have been visiting in these pages. Our lives are not apt to put us in the position of Robin Hood or Dietrich Bonhoeffer. We are too blessed. Their collective example, though, can inspire us to do *something* with our lives besides work and play.

Those "unsung" heroes who take active roles in the causes inspired by people like Catherine and William Booth have got it right, however. It is better to engage a cause than to spend the repetitive evenings watching television. Even tilting at windmills is better than letting life run out meaninglessly. Three cheers for the volunteers, for Habitat for Humanity, for the SPCA and World Vision, and for the Salvation Army.

CHAPTER 27

Mary Slessor: Missionary Hero, (and White Queen of Calabar)

In a rain of poison arrows at the hands of Auca Indians, five young men died in Ecuador in 1957. They were missionaries, who had devoted their lives to taking the Gospel and the practical message of God's love to the extremities of the earth. Elizabeth Eliot, widow of one of the young martyrs, told their story in *Through Gates of Splendor*. Eliot and other widows and mothers went back to live among the Amazon tribe that had murdered their husbands.

Since the time of St. Paul, men and women have followed Christ's commandment to carry the Good News into all the world. In our own generation, no missionary has been so well-known or widely beloved as Mother Teresa. The feisty, tiny Albanian nun spent her life in the fetid, endless slums of Calcutta, devoting her life to, in her words: "the hungry, the naked, the homeless, the crippled, the blind, the lepers, all those people who feel unwanted, unloved, uncared for throughout society, people that have become a burden to the society and are shunned by everyone." The order she founded in 1950, the Missionaries of Charity, now numbers some 4,000 men and women throughout the world, carrying on the ministry she began and inspired.

In our contemporary world, there is something suspect about the idea of Christian missions. Taking Western ways and values and an unfamiliar religion to non-Christian peoples is seen as cultural imperialism. Perhaps it is. As Christians of every description and denomination around the world will acknowledge, however, the prime directive of the Church is the Great Commission: to carry the news of God's love and to demonstrate that love in practical ways to a needy world.

By no means are all missionaries saints and heroes. Still, it takes a particular kind of courage to commit yourself to such a life, whether it be serving in the dirty ghettos of urban India, the Amazon rainforest, or the streets of Chicago. Apart from the challenges of ministry and a constant stream of physical and spiritual needs to be ameliorated, missionaries face intense emotional challenges as well. Supported by the Church, they exist without financial security themselves and with never more than will meet their needs. Society is generally indifferent and sometimes actively hostile to their work, and even family and friends may well not understand what motivates their lives.

Leaving family, friends and the comforts of home behind, however, there have always been those who have answered a call within them to carry the message of God's peace and salvation.

In the 21st century, the internet, GPS, cell phones and radio technology guarantees that anywhere in the world is in nearly instant *contact* with home at least. And our aeronautic age can bring us from Kuala Lumpur to Philadelphia in a matter of hours. How different it would have been when leaving home meant leaving with no return and no contact for years, decades—or life. So it was for the White Queen of Calabar.

A diminutive and timid young woman with a great sense of purpose, Mary Slessor was among many in Scotland moved with missionary zeal by the news of David Livingstone's death. Having been accepted by the Foreign Mission Board, at age 28 she set sail by herself from Liverpool in August 1876 aboard a steamer bound for Nigeria with a cargo of rum. Her destination was Calabar, the West African jungles of headhunters, cannibalism and slave trading.

Mary Slessor landed in a settlement of barracoons, where captives were penned awaiting the slave ships. This was a very different world from the drawing rooms of her native Aberdeen. In this land, guilt or innocence was determined by trial through poison; on the death of a chief, multiple wives were slain to accompany his spirit; village chiefs could order a score of beheadings for a cannibalistic feast; newborn twins were tossed out into the jungle as bad luck; tribal wars were motivated by the slave trade; human life was degraded and cheap. The land was Equatorial Africa. Behind the narrow Atlantic strand of coastline, the wet jungle teemed with disease, predatory reptiles and carnivorous mammals. Mary Slessor went into this world alone.

She began to rescue abandoned twin babies and to learn Efik, the language of the Calabar people. In a land of cruelty, barbarism and physical hostility, Mary Slessor began to live out her faith in the most practical of ways. Mary pushed on into the interior of present-day Nigeria not quite by herself; she took her new family of five native orphans, the oldest a boy of 11; the youngest she carried in her arms. They traveled upriver by canoe, then trekked four miles through the rainforest after dark to the village of Ekenge. Acknowledging the determined lady's courage, the village chief let her stay. She built a mud hut for her young family. She went barefoot, slept on the ground, ate the food and drank the water of the people. It was a regimen that would have intimidated the toughest *Survivor* competitors, and should by rights have killed her.

Mary Slessor made her life among the people of Ekenge, treating their disease and wounds from her limited medical supplies and knowledge, and adding to her family of orphans from the outcasts of tribal life. The reputation of the white Ma spread through the region. When a chief in another district lay near dying, she was frantically summoned by his harem, who feared for their own lives if the chief died. She immediately walked through 8 miles of jungle to his side; when Mary's nursing and medicine brought the chief to health, she became something of a celebrity among the Calabar people.

As the years passed, Mary Slessor moved deeper into the interior, taking her growing family with her. She adopted and loved 25-30 orphans at a time, caring for them herself in houses she constructed each time she moved. She nursed a village through a smallpox epidemic, burying the dead herself. She literally walked in between native armies adrenalin-pumped for war and forced them to make peace. Ma Slessor became judge and peacemaker throughout the region, rescued hundreds of babies deserted to die in the jungles, prevented many local wars, stopped the practice of the poison ordeal and organized churches as a witness to the God of love who motivated her life.

Though she did return to visit Scotland, for 40 years Mary Slessor lived and labored for her Lord in Nigeria. She survived dysentery and fevers of every description, far from her home and the comforts of Aberdeen, to bring light and life to a dark and dangerous place. On her deathbed in January 1915, Ma Slessor, revered by now as the White Queen of Calabar, lay surrounded by her twins, the adult children she had rescued as infants and adopted as her own.

It is one of those things that you either get or you don't. If you are not a person of faith, you might well appreciate the positive results for quality of human life that Mary Slessor accomplished during four decades in East Africa without her life story resonating very much personally. For Believers, however, Ma is a hero, and the heart of her story lies in her motivation rather than in her results.

CHAPTER 28

Eric Liddell: The Moral Hero

"God made me fast. And when I run, I feel his pleasure."

O ne face of heroism is the heroism of conscience. Many of our heroes have been bound by their conscience. Among the noblest and most difficult of human postures is to be faithful to a conviction of right, not in the face of "wrong," but in opposition to what is generally accepted as the right by society. Such was the position faced by young Eric Liddell in the 1924 Olympic Games in Paris.

Liddell's story is well-known today, thanks in no small part to its retelling in the 1981 Best Picture Academy-Award winning movie *Chariots of Fire*. Born in Tianjin, Northern China to Scottish missionary parents of the London Mission Society, Eric Liddell was sent to England at age six, where he and his brother, Rob, were schooled at Eltham College, Blackheath. Both the Liddell brothers were outstanding athletes, but the lad who would become known as the "Flying Scotsman" was exceptional.

At Eltham, Eric Liddell played for both the 1st XI and the 1st XV at age 15, later captaining both those cricket and rugby teams. His triumphs on the track, however, gave him a reputation as Scotland's fastest runner and a potential Olympic contender.

In 1920, Eric followed his brother north to the University of Edinburgh. While studying Pure Science, Liddell played rugby for the University and for the Scottish national team. He also ran the 100 yard and 200 yard dashes for the University—vanquishing all who ran against him. In July 1923, Liddell won both events at the AAA Championships in London. He won the Harvey Cup as best athlete of the meet, and his English record in the 100 stood for 35 years.

By this time, Eric Liddell was a popular national sports figure, and a Scottish hero to a nation that had never won Olympic gold before. The unassuming runner was also known for his Christian faith and willingness to share that faith with others. He had an unshakeable confidence that God supported him in every way and guided his running.

Liddell prepared for the 1924 Olympics in Paris as a favorite in the 100-meter dash and a strong contender in the 200. Famously, when he found out the heats for the 100 were on Sunday, Liddell withdrew from the race. It was his belief that Sunday was the Lord's Day—to be given to God and not to sport. In the face of public dismay and disbelief, conflict within and pressure from without, Liddell honored his conviction. Fame, glory and the pride of accomplishment Liddell sacrificed, not in the face of anonymity, but in the face of public ignominy.

After winning a bronze medal in the 200, Liddell raced his way through the 400-meter heats. He was not expected to win. In the event, the Flying Scotsman ran to victory and a world record time of 47.6 seconds. Eric Liddell had his gold medal and became a national hero.

After completing his degree at Edinburgh, Liddell returned the next year to China, following his parents to the mission field. Liddell taught in the Anglo-Chinese College, coached and taught sports and ran a Sunday School. He married the daughter of Canadian missionaries and fathered three daughters.

In 1941 with the Sino-Japanese War causing chaos in China, British nationals were advised to leave. While he sent his wife and children to Canada, Liddell himself stayed on, to work at a rural mission station in Siaochang where his brother was a doctor. When the fighting reached Siaochang in March 1943, the Japanese committed Liddell to the Weihsien Internment Camp. With a brain tumor aggravated by malnourishment and overwork, Liddell died in the camp in January 1945.

Eric Liddell's heroism was accomplished when he displayed the courage to live by the precepts to which he claimed adherence. He practiced what he preached. In the face of public outcry, disapproval and misunderstanding, Liddell took a determined but widely unpopular stand. If the story ended there, he would be as heroic a man as he is regarded today.

Liddell could have returned to Morningside Congregational, his Edinburgh kirk, to his mission and to China, and he would have been admired all his days for the stand of conscience he had taken. But he would be very much a forgotten hero now. After all, it was not for his stand of conscience that he was crowned with laurels and paraded through the streets. It was for unexpectedly and heroically winning the gold in the 400-meter race that sealed his heroism with fame.

That gold medal, won under adversity, however, obscures the inner struggle that Liddell must have faced. Every hero of conscience, whatever the circumstances and details, emerges to decision and action only because of painful emotional and intellectual conflict.

In *Murder in the Cathedral*, T.S. Eliot paints out in detail the conflict undergone by Thomas Becket, the Archbishop of Canterbury being faced with martyrdom at the hands of Henry II's renegade knights. As Becket ponders what to do, he faces the Tempters—holding out the prospects of power, wealth and acclaim in return for sacrificing his conscience. The last Tempter, however, encourages Becket to embrace his martyrdom and revel in the eternal fame, glory and adoration that he will have earned. As Eliot's hero summarizes:

> *"The last temptation is the greatest treason:*
> *To do the right deed for the wrong reason."*

Perhaps, for example, Liddell doubted himself. Perhaps he felt the pressure of the great expectations of a nation weighing upon him. What if he *lost* in that 100-meter trial? There are plenty of athletes who know what it feels like to be the goat. To blow it on the free-throw line in the last seconds. To strike out with the bases loaded and two out in the ninth. To drop the catch in the end zone as time runs out. What would happen if Liddell had actually failed in that 100-meter sprint he was favored to win? Of course, you cannot lose if you don't run. Here was an out. He could claim the crisis of conscience and accept a kind of martyrdom that would result in at worst a grudging admiration from all, and real adoration from his coreligionists.

No, that's not the sort of man Eric Liddell was— as the rest of his life bears witness. He took on the challenge of the 400-meter, under prepared and with lowered expectations. That he would take it that seriously in the face of having given up his best event under such circumstances is in itself indicative of his competitive heart and character. That he won just makes the story more fun.

Though commercial opportunities in the 1920s were not what they are today, with Liddell's national celebrity, athletic prowess and education, surely the Flying Scotsman could have organized a fairly cushy life for himself in Edinburgh or London.

As it happens, Liddell's convictions regarding sports on the Lord's Day relaxed. Later in life, he refereed youth soccer matches on Sunday.

CHAPTER 29

Dietrich Bonhoeffer: The Hero of Conscience

"We must learn to regard people less in light of what they do or omit to do, and more in the light of what they suffer."

With Robin Hood and Huck Finn as paradigms, it is easy to see that heroes do sometimes fall outside of the law. Despite our respect for the institutional law, the heroes champion in Robin Hood equity and in Huck moral right or natural law. Sometimes, in fact, the law puts a person in such a position that the crisis of conscience comes passively.

If the law of governments is sometimes not fair and sometimes not morally right, sometimes it is downright evil. That the statue law of a government does not in and of itself describe what we as individuals *ought* to do is illustrated clearly with Nazi Germany. The law of the Reichstag and the Fuehrer, in fact, often bound men and women to collude in cruel injustices against moral right and civil dignity. The barbarous Holocaust, that cold-blooded, systematic campaign of genocide against the Jews of Europe, is but the most widely known today of the perversions of human dignity the German people endured under the Nazi law from 1932 until World War II's end in 1945. It does not take long to read that story in Elie Wiesel's *Night* or *The Diary of Anne Frank*.

In one sense, living under Nazi Germany might not have been any different than living under England's Norman oligarchy or any other totalitarian and inhumane regime throughout history. Most people who have ever lived, in fact, have lived their lives under power of a law that did not have as its aim either equity or moral right. As Tolstoy's famous opening line to *Anna Karenina* recounts, however, "All happy families are alike. Each unhappy family is unhappy in its own way." Each autocratic government has its own unjustifiable characteristics that condition the life of its people and that push a few among them in various ways toward that moment when they become a hero.

A unique and fiendish characteristic of Nazism was its unprecedented and brilliant use of propaganda. A small cadre of Hitler loyalists, directed by Joseph Goebbels, actually managed to brainwash tens of millions of people into ignoring and perverting their understanding of right and wrong. That the *law* was on their side was hardly an acceptable defense at the Nuremburg Tribunals.

To run afoul of the law of Nazi Germany, however, was generally more serious than running a stop sign in the wastes of the Arizona desert. They just killed people they didn't like. Just because they did not like them. And you were never sure who *they* was.

As the Nazi hold on German society tightened throughout the 1930s, its tentacles stretched into the German Lutheran church. A church leadership more interested in being German than Christian suborned the Church's allegiance to the historic tenets of Christianity by a variety of rationalizations. Millions of church-going nominal German Lutherans unquestionably *knew* that the *sturm und drang* of Nazism stood in fundamental opposition to their putative Christianity. Between the omnipresent bombardment of National Socialist propaganda, however, and the oppressive miasma of fear, it was not hard to suppress their individual conscience and mold themselves into a collective conformity. Because you were never sure who *they* was.

A small number of Lutheran Christians, however, did maintain an open and spiritual resistance to the anti-gospel of Hitler and his minions. They became known as the Confessing Church. Along with the eminent 20th-century theologian Karl Barth, among their leaders was a young pastor and teacher, Dietrich Bonhoeffer.

Bonhoeffer was born in Breslau, a piece of Germany now in Poland. He determined to become a minister when he was young, went to university at Tubingen and received his doctorate in theology from the University of Berlin when he was 21. He was ordained and spent a year in post-grad work at Union Theological Seminary in New York. It was not long after he returned to the University of Berlin to teach theology and write before the Nazis came to power. In 1933, Bonhoeffer left Germany to pastor in London. In the spring of 1935, however, he returned to assume the leadership of the Confessing Church's illegal seminary. Outspoken in his opposition to Nazi persecution of the Jews, Bonhoeffer was banned finally from teaching and speaking by the Gestapo.

Some individuals seem wired by nature or nurture to go seek the kind of life experience that propels them toward heroism—Lord Nelson, Captain Cook, MacArthur; other heroes unselfconsciously spring to life in moments of reaction to something thrust upon them. Still others go about the business of life and find themselves stuck in a situation that *forces* them to make a self-denying decision of conscience. In the mid-1930s, Bonhoeffer had been a Christian pacifist. In 1939, however, he joined a cadre of Abwehr officers in a plot to assassinate Hitler and overthrow the Nazi regime.

Bonhoeffer was arrested in early 1943 for his role helping Jews escape to Switzerland. For almost two years, he was imprisoned in Berlin and a string of prison camps. After his connection with the Abwehr conspiracy was discovered, Bonhoeffer's fate was sealed. The young Lutheran pastor was hanged at Flossenburg concentration camp in April 1945, just weeks before its liberation. Four members of his immediate family died for their involvement in the small Protestant resistance. In one of his most well-known books, *The Cost of Discipleship*, written in 1937, Dietrich Bonhoeffer wrote: "When Christ calls a man, he bids him come and die."

History is full of men and women who have died for their belief. As ignominious as the reality is, in our own time we have witnessed repeatedly the willingness of Muslim jihadists to die for *their* beliefs. The honor roll of Christian martyrs stretches back to the early disciples of Jesus Christ whose allegiance to "the unknown God" scandalized the Roman world. Civilized Rome fed some of those accused of Christ to the starved beasts let loose in public entertainments.

While religion has certainly prompted its share of martyrs over the centuries, political and social ideals have their heroes of faith as well. In the late 1930s, the Spanish Civil War drew volunteers from across Europe who fought and died for both sides in that grizzly ideological struggle between General Franco's fascists and the communist Republicans. In the grand musical adaptation of Victor Hugo's *Les Miserables* idealistic students rally to the Paris barricades following Enjolras impassioned anthem "Do You Hear the People Sing?" A desolate Marius mourns their deaths over "Empty Chairs at Empty Tables." It was idealists as well who died in Tienemen Square, on the streets of Moscow in 1917 and in the jungles of Guyana with Jim Jones. Whether we approve or agree with their ideals or not, they put themselves on the line.

In one way, like Dietrich Bonhoeffer, we are defined by what we are willing to die for, and by what we are not.

CHAPTER 30

Billy Graham: The Faithful Hero

"My one purpose in life is to help people find a personal relationship with God, which, I believe, comes through knowing Christ."

There is something to be said for faithfulness. These days, it seems rare to find an individual who has heard a clear and strong calling for their life and been single-mindedly true to that calling year after year, decade after decade. We appear to have lost touch with a sense of vocation both in our spiritual lives and in our work.

In our jobs, in our home lives, in the patterns of how we move around the country, we are a restless people these days. We chase the greener grass that always lies on the other side of the next fence. We change homes, communities and states to better ourselves, to move up the career ladder, to be closer to our children or parents, to start over, and over again.

Just so, we are spiritually restless. Compared to past generations, fewer of us really Believe and fewer of us attend church. The essentially Christian world view that served as an invisible hand over American social values has evaporated considerably since World War II. Whether that is a bad thing or a good thing, of course, depends upon who you ask. Still, into the vacuum left by its departure has come witchcraft and New Age paganism, pseudo-science, spirituality without belief, possession worship, pseudo-Christian charlatanism and an array of beliefs that seem nonsensical in the light of 21st century science and social development. People make religion of the darnedest things these days.

The one constant, unchanging Christian voice that a broad American public heard across almost seven decades since World War II was Billy Graham's.

Graham grew up on a dairy farm in Charlotte, North Carolina during the Depression. As a teenager he made a personal commitment to Christ that gave him a direction, a vocation and a calling in life to which he remained true for more than 70 years. He went to Bible school in Florida, college in Illinois and was ordained a Southern Baptist. After serving briefly as a pastor, he joined Youth for Christ. After the war, Graham traveled the United States and Europe as a young evangelist.

An evangelistic crusade in Los Angeles in 1949 brought Billy Graham to international fame. Originally scheduled for three weeks, overflow crowds every night to hear the youthful preacher caused the meetings to be extended to eight weeks. In London, his crusade lasted 12 weeks, and unfathomable as it sounds now, in Graham's New York crusade in 1957, he preached nightly in Madison Square Garden for 16 weeks.

Over the years, Billy Graham traveled the globe proclaiming Jesus Christ. From African villagers and

Australian bushmen to crowned heads of state, Graham delivered the same message to all. He has, quite simply, preached the Christian gospel to more people than anyone else in history—210 million people in 185 countries. Countless more heard him on the weekly "Hour of Decision" radio program over 50 years, and through television, videos and film.

In the process, Graham wrote 25 books, many of which have sold in the millions, and a regular syndicated newspaper column, "My Answer." Since 1950, he directed the vast activity of the Billy Graham Evangelistic Association, which included *Decision* magazine, World Wide Pictures, and the equally world-wide preaching ministry of associate evangelists. And he was the unofficial chaplain to Presidents from the days of Eisenhower.

How Graham has been honored is no less remarkable than his exceptional ministry itself. We might justifiable expect Graham for his life and work to be cheered by the church community—lauded by parachurch organizations and the National Religious Broadcasters and given numerous honorary degrees from Christian colleges and universities. Other accolades he has received, however, bear witness to a man who has lived the Gospel, not merely preached it.

In 1964, Graham received the Gold Award of the George Washington Carver Memorial Institute for his contribution to race relations. In 1966, he accepted the Big Brother of the Year Award at the White House for his contribution to the welfare of children. The Anti-Defamation League of the B'nai Brith in 1969 and the National Conference of Christians and Jews in 1971 recognized him for his efforts to promote interfaith understanding, and in 1977 the American Jewish Committee awarded him their First National Interreligious Award.

Among Billy Graham's profusion of other honors, he has received the Distinguished Service Award from the National Association of Broadcasters (1972), the Templeton Foundation Prize for Progress in Religion (1982), the Presidential Medal of Freedom (1983) and the Congressional Gold Medal (1996). Queen Elizabeth II made him an honorary Knight Commander of the British Empire in 2001 for his international contribution to civic and religious life.

The highest award of all, however, is the honor of a people. Billy Graham was the man most admired by Americans for over 40 years, having appeared 48 times on the annual Gallop Poll's list of "Ten Most Admired Men in the World." No one sets out in their life to achieve such an extraordinary track record of accomplish and honors, certainly not Billy Graham as a kid back on a Carolina dairy farm.

It all came about as the unintended by-product of faithfulness. In two ways is this particular servant of God most noteworthy. First, he never became sidetracked from his original calling. He never changed careers, capitalized on his fame with a commercial sideline, went into politics or doubted his vocation. The message and the messenger remained on focus and unaltered by religious or social fashion. Second, he lived the Christian life he taught. No scandal or taint in money or morals ever compromised his ministry or his effectiveness. No meanness of spirit, self-righteousness or self-promotion ever clouded his message.

It is impossible to know how many lives have been changed by the ministry of Billy Graham. Certainly, for many, the religious high experienced in a crusade meeting or church service does not translate into a continuing or deepened faith in God. Numberless others, however, encountered God for the first time under the preaching of Billy Graham and have gone on to lives of service and ministry themselves. It is these lives, and not the honors, that is Graham's legacy. Well done, thou good and faithful servant.

Faith heroes become heroes because of their faithfulness. In some cases, their faith has cost them their life; in others, it has caused them to spend it. Billy Graham has been a model for many who would preach the Christian gospel and for many who would lead a Christian life. In truth, though, we need not look to the world stage for such models. They are all around us who exhibit faithfulness by their lives, using the gifts they have in modest, consistent ways. In a church setting, they might be pastoring small, rural parishes, teaching Sunday School year after year or keeping an outreach ministry alive with their passion.

But faithfulness too can find its expression in any avenue of life—sweeping the factory floor, caring for the elderly, running an insurance office or building houses. All can serve to remind us that we make a vocation of our own lives, and we find a calling by listening within.

CHAPTER 31

Bartholomew Gosnold: Unsung Hero and Forgotten Founding Father

If a hero is a hero not in any absolute terms, but in the eye of the beholder, then being a "hero" is a social designation, not an intrinsic quality. Can heroism be heroism even if no one knows about the heroic act or individual? Does being a hero require an audience? Unquestionably there are lost to history or to memory many acts and names that would be lauded as heroic if they were known. Like angels unawares there are people who have quietly inhabited our world and have contributed in their own way to defining the society to which we aspire.

Still, after 400 years it is astonishing that America can rediscover a lost hero, a man who perhaps more than any other single individual is responsible for the establishment of British North America, a man whom history ought to have recognized in one sense as the Founding Father of

America. If ever there has been an unsung hero, that would be Bartholomew Gosnold.

Born in 1571 near Ipswich, Suffolk, Bartholomew Gosnold came from the manorial class of a family that traveled in the orbit of the Earl of Essex. Gosnold was sent to Cambridge University and then to London to study law at the Middle Temple, preparing, no doubt, for a career as a country gentleman. Somewhere along the way, however, Gosnold became fascinated by the sea, and in particular by the stories drifting back to England from early voyages to the New World.

Apparently, Gosnold's uncle, Lord of the Manor of Otley, got Gosnold aboard the Earl of Essex's expedition to the Azores in 1597. Then, for a year or so, Gosnold joined Essex in privateering against the Spanish. He made himself something of a small fortune in a short period of time. Gosnold sailed to the New World first with Sir Walter Raleigh on the failed attempt to start a colony at Roanoke.

Thereafter, Gosnold began a campaign to start a colony further north. His old patron Essex got himself beheaded in an abortive palace coup against Queen Elizabeth, but Gosnold succeeded in winning support from the Earl of Southampton. By 1602, the expedition was ready to set sail, in a single vessel, *Concord*, captained by Bartholomew Gosnold. There were 32 on board, with a dozen putative settlers of this new colony. Gosnold pioneered a more northern route across the Atlantic instead of sailing south of the Azores before turning West as was customary. They made the crossing in seven weeks, making landfall at Cape Elizabeth, off what is now Portland, Maine.

Gosnold and the *Concord* sailed south in search of a propitious settlement site. When they traced the peninsula that is Cape Cod, Gosnold named it for the profusion of cod in the surrounding waters. South of the cape, they found the islands. Martha's Vineyard was named for the abundance of wild grapes, and for Bartholomew Gosnold's first-born daughter. The island now called Cuttyhunk Gosnold named Elizabeth's Island after the Queen. There, the party landed and built a fort. Encountering hostile Indians and realizing that they lacked provisions to last until they would be resupplied, however, a month later the would-be settlers abandoned the nascent settlement. Gosnold returned to England with a cargo of cedar and sassafras, his hopes for colonization in the New World undeterred.

For the next several years, Gosnold promoted and schemed to get another colonial voyage organized. In 1603, the death of the aged Queen brought a new dynasty to the throne in the Scottish monarch James I. The new King James brought not only a new circle of power to London, but emboldened new economic ventures as well. From the family's Sussex seat at Otley Hall, Gosnold recruited supporters, patrons and colonists to his venture, including Edward-Maria Wingfield and John Smith. By 1606 planning was completed and the Virginia Company was born.

That December the three-ship fleet set sail from London. The company included 104 settlers (all men) and 55 crewmen. Presumably to separate authority for the voyage from the governance of the colony, Christopher Newport was named Admiral, aboard the *Susan Constant;* Vice Admiral Gosnold commanded the *Godspeed.* He would stay with the colony, while Newport was returning to England.

In late April the fleet arrived in the lower regions of Chesapeake Bay near the mouth of the James River. The company opened their sealed instructions that named a seven-member Council, which would elect its own president who would be Governor for the Crown. Bartholomew Gosnold's name was first on the list.

The island of present-day Jamestown was the site chosen for the settlement. Through the spring, the company erected a triangular fort. Through the early summer, they fought off the local Powhatan Indians. Bartholomew Gosnold is credited with winning a battle against an attack of some 400 Indians by mounting the *Godspeed* and scattering the attack with its heavy cannon.

By August the colonists were beginning to die. The wet, low-lying, mosquito-infested island was rife with dysentery and swamp fever. Malnutrition, high humidity and temperatures in the 90s week after week began to carry them off. Fifty of the 104 settlers died that summer. Bartholomew Gosnold died in late August. He was given a funeral with full military honors in accordance with his rank. And forgotten.

It's pretty clear now that through those difficult summer months in Jamestown, though Wingfield had been given the role of Governor, Gosnold was the *de facto* leader of the settlement. On his death, Wingfield was deposed and ultimately John Smith became Governor. Being a leader by nature and something of a self-promoter, Smith has gone down in the history books as the bright light in the disaster that was the early Jamestown colony. In his own accounts, however, Smith justly gives the credit for the Virginia settlement where it belongs: "Captaine Bartholomew Gosnold, the first mover of this plantation, having many years solicited many of his friends, but found small assistance, at last prevailed with some Gentlemen, as Maister Edward Maria Wingfield, Captaine John Smith, and divers others, who depended a yeare upon his projects...."

There has never been a lack of corroborative evidence detailing the roles Bartholomew Gosnold played in the foundation of what would become British colonial America. Thirteen years after his death, the *Mayflower* would follow the northern route across the North Atlantic that Gosnold pioneered, following his charts into Cape Cod Bay. Finally, after three decades of struggle in the fetid climate of the tidewater, Jamestown and subsequently Virginia would thrive under the governorship of William Berkeley in the 1640s-60s.

Yet Gosnold has remained forgotten. No great rivers bear his name, nor great cities, nor great universities. We never read about him in school, or heard his name numbered among the Founding Fathers.

Gosnold had an idea, a dream and the persistence, luck and connections to make good on that dream. Jamestown was a very shaky proposition for many years. It was very poorly sited, even by the knowledge of the day, and weakly conceived as a society and a colony. Still, it did manage to survive, and go on to celebrate its 400th anniversary as the first permanent colony in British North America and what became these United States. Its founder was Bartholomew Gosnold. We have certainly recognized many national heroes for less significant contributions to our national history.

CHAPTER 32

Booker T. Washington: The Teacher Hero

"If you want to lift yourself up, lift up someone else."

Almost all of us have a teacher in our past who makes an appearance on our roster of personal heroes. It might be a grade school teacher who took us under her wing or who awakened new interests. It might be a high school teacher who opened a love of learning or conveyed a passion for drama, music or science, or a college prof who directed us on a career path. As in any profession, there is plenty of mediocrity in teaching. It is a profession, though, that can make personal heroes, because it changes lives directly.

A whole genre of literature and film celebrates the dedicated teacher who became the personal hero—stories like *To Sir, With Love*, *Educating Rita*, *Stand and Deliver* and *Goodbye, Mr. Chips*. In real life, such great teachers range from Socrates and John Wycliffe to George Washington Carver, Louis Agassiz and Christa MacAuliffe.

From the earliest days of the Puritan colonies of New England, America has been a land where education could create a better way of life for people than their parents experienced. Generations of in-migrations to this country from across the globe have found in education the way to economic and personal success. Education has been the flame under the melting pot. First and second-generation immigrants have always known this, and sacrificed to get their children the education that American society, uniquely in the world, afforded.

African Americans, however, did not willingly seek these shores as an immigrant group. The emancipation from slavery with the Civil War may have been a measure of freedom, but it hardly brought access to the American dream, nor did it bring access to the means of achieving it—education.

When I was a kid, I devoured a series of children's books called "The Childhood of Famous Americans" series. It gave me many early heroes who have followed me through the years. One of the most memorable was Booker T. Washington.

Born into slavery in the piedmont of southwest Virginia in 1856, Washington's emancipated family was poverty stricken following the Civil War. He went to work at age nine as a salt-packer to help his family, and a year later was mining coal in West Virginia. He ended up a houseboy for the mine owner's wife, who recognized Washington's intelligence and encouraged his education. At 16, Washington entered Hampton Institute. Since his parents had no money to help him, the eager teenager walked the 200 miles to the school and paid his way by working as the janitor.

The principal at Hampton, Samuel Armstrong, became a mentor to Washington, instilling in him an education where character and morality counted for much. Armstrong also emphasized the importance of a practical education for African Americans. The post-Reconstruction South was a world of legalized oppression for black Americans. Freedom from slavery brought no ready means for African Americans to improve themselves economically or to gain employment skills.

Washington became dedicated to the idea that education was the means of raising African Americans to full equality. After graduating from school, Washington returned to his Virginia hometown to teach. Then, Armstrong brought him back to teach in Hampton Institute. When a new school for African Americans was being opened in Tuskegee, Alabama in 1881, on Armstrong's recommendation, Booker T. Washington was given charge. Tuskegee Institute opened in a shanty building owned by a local AME Zion church.

Washington did not let it stay there. By 1888, the school had more than 400 students and owned more than 500 acres of land. Tuskegee taught academic subjects, but its emphasis was on practical education in agriculture, building trades and crafts such as printing and shoemaking. The students themselves built the school as it grew. Washington crisscrossed the country campaigning for Tuskegee Institute and raising money.

The Institute thrived and Washington became a nationally known speaker. In 1895, he was invited to speak at the opening of the Cotton States Exposition in Atlanta. President McKinley visited Tuskegee and philanthropist Andrew Carnegie and others donated heavily to the school. In 1900, Washington helped found and became the first president of the National Negro Business League.

More than a generation now has passed since the Civil Rights Bill of 1964 and the Voting Rights Act of 1965. There are grandparents now, black and white, who do not know what the country, particularly the South, was like for African Americans before those turbulent years of the 1960s. Contesting for civil rights and for human dignity remains an ongoing process with no end in sight for a multitude of ethnic, cultural and racial minorities. America is unquestionably the Great Melting Pot, but all the ingredients in the pot don't melt equally fast and don't mix with equal ease.

In his own time, Booker T. Washington was a controversial figure among African Americans and remains so to this day. His accommodationist philosophy rubbed against the grain of those who actively struggled and campaigned for full legal and civil rights in the post-Reconstruction South.

In his 1901 autobiography *Up from Slavery*, Washington wrote: "I believe it is the duty of the Negro ... to deport himself modestly in regard of political claims, depending upon the slow but sure influences that proceed from the possessions of property, intelligence, and high character for the full recognition of his political rights. I think that the according of the full exercise of political rights is going to be a matter of natural, slow growth, not an overnight gourdvine affair."

It is easy now from the distance of more than a century to second-guess the compromises that Washington willingly accepted in the South of those years. Against the criticism and enmity of both black activists and southern white racists, Washington stood his ground and became the counselor of presidents. In due course, he proved prophetic. The full exercise of political rights for African Americans did not come without struggle when it finally *did* come. Unquestionably, however, the way was paved by generations of Tuskegee students who became early leaders in the development of the black community across the South.

The Jamestown Festival of 1907 brought landmark celebrations marking the tercentennial of the founding of Jamestown colony in 1607—America's 300th birthday by some reckoning. Amidst the parades, reviews and sundry events, the headline speakers keynoting the celebrations were President Teddy Roosevelt, Mark Twain and Booker T. Washington.

Washington remained at the helm of Tuskegee Institute (what has been since 1985 Tuskegee University) until his death in 1915. By then, the school had grown from a one-room shanty to an institution with 1,500 students and 200 faculty. It offered 40 "trades" or majors on a 100-building campus and had a two-million-dollar endowment. After a funeral attended by a crowd of more than 8,000, Booker T. Washington was buried near the University Chapel.

A monument to Washington erected in 1922 and titled "Lifting the Veil" stands at the center of the Tuskegee campus. Its inscription reads, "He lifted the veil of ignorance from his people and pointed the way to progress through education and industry."

There are thousands of teachers in inner city schools, anonymous suburbs and high schools handicapped by rural poverty who labor in anonymity, but light the spark in their students that will never be forgotten. In the legacy of Booker T. Washington, we are reminded how they can change lives.

CHAPTER 33

Teddy Roosevelt: Presidential Hero

"Far better it is to dare mighty things, to win glorious triumphs, even though checkered by failure, than to take rank with those poor spirits who neither enjoy much nor suffer much, because they live in the gray twilight that knows neither victory nor defeat."

Every four-year presidential campaign cycle brings with it a predictable parade of questions that we ask of candidates for the office of Head of State and Head of Government. Among other things, we ask whether a candidate is "Presidential." In appearance, demeanor, personality and accomplishment, there seems to be a Platonic ideal against which we measure potential presidents.

I have spent most of my life in New Hampshire, where presidential politics are the official state sport. With New Hampshire's first-in-the-nation presidential primary, it is the one state in the Union where there is no political off-season. Though New Hampshire is a small state, it has the largest state legislature in the country. *Everyone* who has lived in the state for any period of time knows one or a few state legislators personally. It is a state of activists, and the candidates, the potential candidates, the testing-the-water candidates and the future candidates for president come to New Hampshire. They talk to the *New Hampshire Union Leader*, the statewide paper, and WMUR ABC-9, the statewide broadcast television channel, and they meet people. Once the race is on, it really is true that any NH voter can easily meet personally any or all of the candidates for president. After witnessing New Hampshire primaries for several decades, I conclude, to little surprise, that . . . the packaging is everything these days.

Candidates who are short and bald have not got a prayer. We would never elect a small man like James Monroe today, or a man as heavy as William Howard Taft. Candidates whose avocations are stamp collecting and knitting do not win delegates to the electoral college either. Academic types do not seem to do well anymore, either. It would be tough for Woodrow Wilson on the campaign trail in our video era.

A candidate has got to look good on television and make a commanding personal appearance. There has to be some charisma in the personality that captures people instantly and can be to some measure communicated both visually and in his or her speaking voice.

We *want* a president to be a hero. At the very least, we want a president who could credibly look and act like a hero if the situation arose. George Washington, Andy Jackson, Zachary Taylor, Abe Lincoln, US Grant: now, *those* were

Presidents—at least in our collective imagination. A president has got to be tough. Not coarse, but rugged in character. Outdoorsmen are preferred, or adventurers in some fashion. A president can not be languorous of temperament, but needs to be quick thinking and determined, a person of action, not merely a person of words.

Who we *want* is Teddy Roosevelt.

When Theodore Roosevelt became the 26th President on the assassination of President McKinley in 1901, he became at 42 the youngest President in history. He had already been a New York Assemblyman, Police Commissioner of New York City, Governor of New York, U.S. Civil Service Commissioner, Colonel of the Rough Riders and Assistant Secretary of the Navy, as well as Vice President. The guy just could not seem to keep a job.

Teddy Roosevelt's is no rags-to-riches story; he came from a wealthy family. His struggle, though, was against a sickly boyhood, and he became an ardent outdoorsman as a result. Roosevelt ranched in the Badlands of Dakota, hunted big game and led major scientific expeditions of many months in South America and Africa.

During the Spanish-American War, Roosevelt led the Rough Rider Regiment of cavalry. At the Battle of San Juan, he led the famous charge that made him one the most popular heroes of the war. He rode that fame to office as Governor of New York, went on to the Vice Presidency and ultimately the White House.

During his tenure in the Presidency from 1901 to 1909, Roosevelt transformed the office of President, expanding executive powers and largely creating the model of the Presidency as we recognize it today. He led Congress and America for the first time onto the world stage of international politics and away from the isolationism that had been an American inclination. Roosevelt's tag line was "Walk softly, but carry a big stick." He built up the Navy so that America would have a Big Stick in the world.

Roosevelt also changed the face of American capitalism, curbing the laissez-faire freedoms of American corporations and ending the strangle hold of trusts and monopolies on the marketplace. This was the "Square Deal" for all Americans that helped millions to earn a living wage. He established the Department of Commerce and Labor. He also regulated the railroads, promoted the Meat Inspection Act, began the Panama Canal and secured passage of the Pure Food and Drug Act.

It was in the area of conservation, however, that Roosevelt may have provided his most lasting legacy. During his years in office, he designated almost 230 million acres of land under federal protection, creating five National Parks, 150 National Forests, 51 Federal Bird Reservations, 18 National Monuments, 21 Reclamation Projects and the first four National Game Preserves. That is as much total land as every East Coast state between Eastport and Key West. He was considered in his day to be the foremost authority on large North American mammals.

While he was not otherwise engaged, Roosevelt mediated international disputes over Venezuela, the Dominican Republic and Morocco. For negotiating the peace concluding the Russo-Japanese War, Roosevelt won the Nobel Peace Prize. And during the Roosevelt presidency, he managed to cut the national debt.

Along the way, Roosevelt authored more than 30 books; he was a founding member of the American Institute of Arts and Letters, President of the American

Historical Association and one of the original honorees elected to the American Academy of Arts and Letters. He was also one of the founders of the NCAA.

Now, *there* is a President. In terms of sheer activity—just getting things done—we shall not see his like again. It is not that there are not men and women of equal ability and ambition in the world today, but the nature of the federal government and real-world politics has changed considerably in the last hundred years. The Executive Branch that Roosevelt governed was just a much smaller government than exists today. In the early 1900s, there were no entitlement programs to administer, fewer cabinet departments and much less governmental bureaucracy. The Legislative branch was more gentlemanly and smaller as well. There were no cameras to play for, no instant communication, no media but newspapers. Today, the process of moving either branch of government to action requires such public scrutiny, grandstanding, political manipulation and posturing for media-fed constituencies that no agenda as broad, swift and decisive as Roosevelt's could be engineered by any President.

No wonder a character like Teddy Roosevelt remains larger than life—the embodiment of the president as hero. Washington, Jefferson and Lincoln each have an iconic identity tied to a particular role in American history. Teddy Roosevelt joins them on the national monument at Mount Rushmore for the sum of his presidential accomplishments.

CHAPTER 34

Alvin York: Reluctant Hero

He was what most of us would call a hillbilly. Alvin York was born in the rural backwater of Fentress County, Tennessee in 1887, in the Valley of the Three Forks of the Wolf. York was third of 11 children in a family of subsistence farmers, eking a hardscrabble living from 75 acres of the inhospitable hills of northeastern Tennessee. The local culture placed little value on education, and York received only a few months of schooling as a boy. What he did learn to do, however, was shoot a rifle with deadly accuracy. Squirrel, quail, deer, raccoon or wild boar: after all, in his world, what you shot was what you ate.

As a young man, Alvin York got something of a reputation as a hell raiser. In 1914, his best friend got killed in a bar fight, however, and York decided he needed to change his life. He had a religious conversion at a revival meeting and became active in the local congregation of a small denomination, the Church of Christ in Christian Union. When the United States entered World War I in 1917, Alvin received his draft notice. His church, however, was pacificist, and York sent back his draft card with the notation: "Don't want to fight." Because the Church of Christ in Christian Union was not recognized as a denomination, York's attempt to claim status as a conscientious objector was disallowed. He went off to Camp Gordon, Georgia, for basic training with great unease of soul.

From the day he received his draft notice until he returned to the hills of Tennessee, York kept a diary. In it, he summarized how he was torn between his faith and his patriotic duty: "So you see my religion and my experience . . . told me not to go to war, and the memory of my ancestors . . . told me to get my gun and go fight. I didn't know what to do. I'm telling you there was a war going on inside me, and I didn't know which side to lean to. I was a heap bothered. It is a most awful thing when the wishes of your God and your country get mixed up and go against each other. One moment I would make up my mind to follow God, and the next I would hesitate and almost make up my mind to follow Uncle Sam. Then I wouldn't know which to follow or what to do. I wanted to follow both but I couldn't. They were opposite. I wanted to be a good Christian and a good American too."

In the end, and with the sympathetic help of his officers, York resolved his conscience and determined that his duty lay in being the best soldier he could be. York went to Europe with the 328th Infantry of the 82nd Division; his company went into the front lines in France at the beginning of the Battle of the Argonne in October 1918.

In the first advance of the battle on October 8th, York, now a corporal, was sent as part of a 17-man squad to take control of a section of railroad behind Hill 223. The men

misread their French map and ended up behind enemy
lines. In the fire fight that followed, nine men in his unit
died. York was ordered to silence the machine gun that
was pinning down them down. The short version is that
he was successful. When the dust settled on Hill 223, the
seven American survivors had captured 132 prisoners. York
never claimed to have done it all himself, but there is no
question that he was the man of the match.

The official dispatch of the 82nd Division to GHQ read:
"The part which Corporal York individually played in the
attack (the capture of the Decauville Railroad) is difficult to
estimate. Practically unassisted he captured 132 Germans
(three of whom were officers), took about 35 machine
guns, and killed no less than 25 of the enemy, later found
by others on the scene of York's extraordinary exploit. The
story has been carefully checked in every possible detail from
headquarters of this division and is entirely substantiated.
Although York's statement tends to underestimate the
desperate odds which he overcame, it has been decided to
forward to higher authorities the account given in his own
name. The success of this assault had a far-reaching effect in
relieving the enemy pressure against American forces in the
heart of the Argonne Forest."

Wars need heroes. They inspire the troops and
warm the hearts of the people back home. York was
duly honored for courage, bravery and accomplishment.
Probably no war ever needed heroes as much as World War
I. Year after year, the pointless slaughter in the European
trenches had drained the manhood of a dozen countries.
Alvin York became the poster boy for the weary victory,
deliberately championed as the war's greatest hero and
feted accordingly.

Most immediately, York was promoted to sergeant. He spent the rest of the month in the battle waged through the Argonne forest. In early November, while he was on a 10-day furlough in France, the Armistice was signed. And as news of his exploit on October 8th had gotten around, Sgt. York found himself to be a celebrity.

For the next six months, York traveled across France making official appearances, speaking to soldiers and receiving honors: the Distinguished Service Cross, the Congressional Medal of Honor and the French *Croix de Guerre*. In awarding the latter, Marshal Foch declared York's action to be "the greatest thing accomplished by any private soldier of all the armies of Europe."

In early May, York finally boarded the *U.S.S. Ohio* in Bordeaux and sailed for home. He received the classic hero's welcome in New York—a ticker tape parade that set a record at the time. He then went to Washington where he was honored at a joint meeting of both houses of Congress. When he finally arrived home in Pall Mall, Tennessee on May 29, 1919, thousands of Tennesseans had gathered along the railroad tracks and the highways to get a glimpse of the local hero and welcome him home.

Alvin York remained self-effacing about his heroic status and shunned the inevitable outpouring of commercial propositions and endorsements that his instant fame brought to him. He was married to his long-time sweetheart, by the governor of Tennessee no less, and settled to life in the valleys of the Wolf River. Though York had always pined to be home in the beloved hills of Tennessee, however, being in the wider world had inevitably changed him. In the cities of America and Europe and the combat trenches, he saw how much the people of his valley home were held back by their lack of education and interaction with the outside world.

York devoted himself to bringing schools to the region, improving roads and opening up the Tennessee hill country to the 20th century. Among his successes was the York Agricultural Institute that the state established in Pall Mall; York Institute continues today as a public high school.

York became politically active in the state and spoke tirelessly for education. He became a vocal member of the Fight for Freedom Committee arguing against the popular isolationism of 1940-41. When World War II finally came to us, York tried to reenlist in the infantry but was denied due to age. He toured the country with the Signal Corps, on recruitment and war bond drives and camp inspections. He became chairman of the Fentress County Draft Board. Later in life, when asked how he wanted to be remembered, York replied that he wanted to be remembered for improving basic education in Tennessee and for helping people.

After 10 years of debilitating illness, Alvin York died in September 1964. As you might expect, he was buried with full military honors. He is buried in the Pall Mall cemetery near the Church of Christ in Christian Union, that is now named York Chapel.

CHAPTER 35

Eleanor Roosevelt: Hero in the Vanguard

*"Surely, in the light of history, it is more intelligent
to hope rather than to fear, to try rather than not
to try. For one thing we know beyond all doubt:
Nothing has ever been achieved by the person who
says, 'It can't be done.'"*

Among the common characteristics that show up in
our heroes is dedication to a cause or ideal. Disparate
heroes like Robin Hood, Harriet Tubman, William
Tyndale and David Ben Gurion all share the attribute
of being wholly consumed by a cause. In most cases, we
know of those heroes today because of their success, not
the valor of the attempt. How many undersung heroes out
there led the way that others followed more famously we
shall never know.

The past two generations of my Yankee ancestors, at
least, would be rolling over in their proverbial graves to
read me lauding Eleanor Roosevelt. The New Deal, FDR

and his ilk did not play too strongly in the Republican small towns of Northern New England back then. Unquestionably Eleanor Roosevelt was a woman who was controversial in her own time (who isn't?). She met the censure she received head on and plowed her own way in the hardscrabble era of the Great Depression, World War II and beyond. As her time became our own, however, Eleanor has proven to have indeed been an early planter of the substantive, positive change in our society that was harvested through the last decades of the 20th century.

She was born Anna Eleanor Roosevelt in 1885, into a silver-spoon New York City family. Her father, Elliott, was Teddy Roosevelt's kid brother. Mom was a beautiful socialite who died when Eleanor was seven. Dad drank himself to death within a couple of years. Eleanor was raised by her grandmother and sent off to London as a teen to a posh English girls' school. They were happy, influential years for her at Allenswood Academy and she returned to New York as a debutante—confident, opinionated and determined to get involved in the world. Eleanor threw herself into the work of a variety of reform agencies such as the National Consumers League and the Junior League, volunteered to teach in the settlement houses and, in 1905, married her fifth cousin, Franklin Delano Roosevelt. Her uncle, President Teddy, gave the bride away.

The Roosevelts' first decade of married life was dominated by childbirth for Eleanor. They had six children born during those years. Franklin was making his way up the ladder in Democratic politics. They moved to Albany in 1911 when FDR was elected to the state senate, and to Washington two years later when he became Assistant Secretary of the Navy in the Wilson administration. By now, Eleanor knew the ins and outs of life as a political wife. She managed both FDR's political persona and their social calendar adroitly. But Eleanor wanted desperately to be her own person: "I wanted to be independent," she recalled decades later. "I was beginning to realize that something within me craved to be an individual."

When World War I came along, Eleanor Roosevelt found the avenue she needed, stirring Washington's notice with the dedication and energy she devoted to Navy Relief and the Red Cross canteen. After Coolidge won the 1920 election, the Roosevelts returned to New York. Eleanor joined the Women's Division of the Democratic State Committee, the Women's City Club, and local chapters of the Women's Trade Union League and the League of Women Voters. She chaired, coordinated, lobbied and arbitrated, tackling issues such as child labor laws, workers compensation and legalizing the distribution of birth control information. Eleanor Roosevelt's life as an activist was just beginning.

Eleanor worked tirelessly for the Democratic party and campaigned for candidates across New York state, building her campaign skills and her own political network. She chaired the women's delegation to the platform committee of the 1924 Democratic National Convention and convinced FDR to run successfully for Governor in 1928.

By now, the Roosevelt marriage had changed. After Eleanor discovered that Franklin had been messing about with her social secretary, they lived a largely political marriage rather than an intimate one. They each had their own political and personal support systems and formed separate strong attachments to friends and co-workers. Eleanor was fulfilled and happy on her own. "It is essential," she maintained, for a woman, "to develop her own interests, to carry on a stimulating life of her own." And she did.

When Eleanor entered the White House with FDR in 1933, she did so with some reluctance, fearing that the expectations put upon a First Lady would limit her personal independence and restrict her ability to champion the causes in which she so ardently believed. Certainly, the social and ceremonial demands upon the president's wife were significant. In characteristic fashion, though, Eleanor took the role way beyond what it had been—becoming the first "modern" First Lady.

Eleanor Roosevelt held her own press conferences and let Washington know from the beginning that she did not intend to be a passive by-stander during her husband's tenure as president. She pressured the FDR administration to appoint women to significant positions in the New Deal programs that transformed Government during the 1930s. She lobbied for anti-poverty programs, pushed for the hiring of minorities and women in federal agencies, and left an imprint on many of the federal programs designed to get us through the difficult years of the Great Depression.

In 1935, Eleanor began a syndicated newspaper column, "My Day," which she wrote for more than 25 years. She also wrote monthly columns variously for *Women's Home Companion*, *Ladies Home Journal* and *McCalls*. She traveled extensively around the country speaking, visiting relief projects and reporting on living and working conditions to the nation and to the President. In short, she became the most effective and ardent spokesperson for the FDR administration's agenda we call the New Deal.

Among the most controversial of Eleanor Roosevelt's causes was her increasing commitment to civil rights. In these days, while we squabble over policy some, the cause of civil rights itself is universally regarded as noble. Such was not the case in the 1930s and 1940s, especially within the heavily Southern Democratic party. She joined the Washington chapter of the NAACP, became the first white to join the DC chapter of the National Urban League and addressed both their national conventions in 1936. Eleanor pressured the government to pay black and white workers equally, co-chaired the National Committee to Abolish the Poll Tax and convened the National Conference of Negro Women at the White House. In her book *The Moral Basis for Democracy*, she trumpeted the theme that civil rights were the litmus test of our democracy.

The First Lady's strong voice for civil rights carried through the difficult years of World War II. She pushed to keep civil rights issues on the political agenda and played a leading role in establishing the Fair Employment Practices Commission.

When FDR died in April 1945, Eleanor returned to her home in Hyde Park, New York. Her active life was hardly over. She continued her daily column and her magazine columns and wrote books. In December 1945, President Harry Truman appointed her to the United States delegation to the United Nations, in which capacity she served until 1953. She campaigned vigorously for support of the UN, chaired the committee that drafted the Universal Declaration of Human Rights and later chaired the Human Rights Commission. President John Kennedy reappointed her in 1961. She also chaired the President's Commission on the Status of Women and served on the national boards of several major civil rights organizations.

Roosevelt was a hero in the vanguard who had a significant impact upon the society in which we live today. The nature of her role and her work, unelected and largely unofficial, means that Eleanor Roosevelt will never play as large in the popular history of the 20th century as she did in her own three decades of national public life. In her lifetime, though, she was recognized 11 years consecutively in Gallup polls as the most admired woman in the world and declared by President Harry Truman to be "First Lady of the World."

CHAPTER 36

Ted Williams: The Sports Hero

Compared to the heroic exploits of warriors and world leaders, sports seems an unlikely arena in which to find true heroes. In fact, however, sports figures have for generations been venerated by youngsters who have sought to emulate their prowess and their stature. How many young basketball players grew up dreaming of Michael Jordan? How many little girls trying to perfect their back round-off can name every one of the U.S. Women's Gymnastic team?

Somehow, however, baseball has always been the sport of heroes. After all, it is the Great American Game. From San Francisco to Baltimore, every major league team has generated its heroes for generations of young people to emulate—Jackie Robinson, Willie Mays and Stan Musial, Derek Jeter and Cal Ripken. Up in Red Sox Nation, amidst the shades of Bobby Doerr, Johnny Pesky, Carl Yazstremski and Carlton Fisk, there is no more legendary hero than the great Ted Williams—arguably the greatest hitter in history.

In Ted Williams' 1939 rookie season with the Red Sox, he won Rookie of the Year honors, with an American League-leading (and rookie record) 145 RBIs. In 1941, he became the last man to hit above .400 for the season. On the last day of the season, Williams average stood exactly at .400. He was offered the chance to protect it by sitting out the double-header that day. He refused and played both games, going 6 for 8 to finish the season at .406. The next year he won the Triple Crown. Not a bad start to a major league career.

But World War II was in progress. Williams left the ball diamond and enlisted in the Naval Air Corps. He was trained as a pilot and commissioned in May 1944 as a naval aviator. Williams served as a staff flight instructor in Pensacola, FL flying F4U Corsairs. After a tour in the Pacific at the end of the war, Williams was relieved of active duty in January 1946 and rejoined the Red Sox for spring training. He had missed three seasons—perhaps those of his career's prime. That year, after having been out of baseball for three years, Williams was the American League MVP. He won the Triple Crown again in 1947, and MVP honors again in 1949.

In early 1952, now Captain Williams was recalled by the Marines for duty in the Korean War. He went to Korea, this time to fly F9 Panther jets. Though Williams always downplayed his combat role in Korea, he flew 39 combat missions and was shot up twice. He was released in July 1953 and got back to Boston to play the last 37 games of the season, hitting .407.

When Williams retired in 1960 at 42, he hit a home run, his 521st, in his last at-bat in Fenway Park. His lifetime batting average of .344 was exceeded only by Ty

Cobb, Rogers Hornsby and Shoeless Joe Jackson. Williams' career .634 slugging percentage is second only to Ruth, and his .483 on-base percentage is the major league record. And he had missed almost five seasons at the peak of his career to serve in WWII and Korea. Now *there's* a sports hero.

Admittedly, Ted Williams was a bit of a curmudgeonly hero; he did not care much for the press or the public relations end of his career. After his retirement, Williams seemed to warm up a bit to his role as a regional hero, and he always enjoyed returning in later life to Fenway to receive the cheers of the crowd. Talk about someone to emulate as a sportsman.

The story could have been of Jackie Robinson, Mike Schmidt or Willie Stargill. Williams is only a chosen icon from the pantheon of baseball greats and sports legends in every other field of athletic endeavor. It is more difficult these days to find sports heroes anywhere. Plenty has been written about the way pro athletes these days are paid extraordinarily irrational sums of money. With free agency, superstars and journeymen alike auctioning themselves to the highest bidder. On the one hand, this is the great American way—a free labor market. *No one* wants to sell their services for less than they are worth in the marketplace. Professional athletes are no different in that way from any of their fans.

In truth, however, the free labor market in sports has made it more difficult to find sports heroes, because we associate sports heroes with their teams. Lou Gehrig was a Yankee. Willie Mays was a Giant. Al Kaline was a Tiger. Hank Aaron was a Brave. Their accomplishments on the field would be no less if they had played for four or five teams during their career. Playing with a single team, however, they built their status with the fan base of a single franchise across three generations, and played their way not only into the record books but into the rarified ranks of popular heroes.

When Cal Ripken broke Lou Gehrig's streak of 2,130 consecutive major league games played, it was one of the memorable sporting moments of history. Baseball fans and sports fans everywhere cheered and admired Ripken's extraordinary effort. The gritty shortstop made his mark, however, as an Oriole. It is to a generation of Baltimore fans that he is a *hero*.

There is always a tradeoff. Loyalty to a team has a cost, and a reward. Every athlete (and their agent) makes a decision. Some 95 percent of free agency athletes in every big-money professional sport make the choice to follow the bigger money. And which of us really can blame them? For better or for worse, free agency and the big money has changed all the professional sports, however, and the way in which athletes are perceived by society.

In every sport there are certainly great athletes who are great human beings—who give of themselves beyond their sport and to their sport beyond their abilities. The changes in sports and in the national culture that enthusiastically supports them, however, cannot detract from the accomplishments of exceptional individual athletes or generation of aspiring ballplayers they inspire.

Ted Williams will aways be a Red Sox icon and a hero to New Englanders.

CHAPTER 37

John Wayne: Playing the Hero

"Nobody should come to the movies unless they believe in heroes."

I n the idyllic countryside of southern England near the village of Flakeham sits the town of Laredo. As you walk out on the streets of Laredo, you will be in a 19th-century town from the American western frontier. Though it has been used for movies, this is not a movie set. Every building is complete, authentically furnished, equipped and inhabited, from the Saloon to the Undertaker's. Enthusiasts populate the town (part-time), living out roles and occupations in a time and culture warp. More than a century and a continent away from 1800s Texas, what a commingling of life and art!

For those of us too young to remember, back in the 1950s and the early 1960s the most popular genre of television show was the Western. For 30 years already, Americans had been dazzled on the silver screen by Westerns starring popular genre actors like Tom Mix,

Gene Autry and Roy Rogers. By the time the Ponderosa appeared in living color in *Bonanza* (1960), it was a well-known canard that you could always tell the good guys because they wear white hats. Amazingly enough, it was generally true. In thousands of Western films and TV shows, the good guys almost always appear in white hats and the bad guys in black hats. Ah, if life were only that simple.

The Western is the quintessential American film genre. And it is a uniquely American genre. It is often noted that America's chief import to the world is popular culture. If this is true, then the baseline of that popular culture and its first defining icon is the Western. Around the globe, America's swashbuckling reputation, open, hardy, loud-spoken and out-spoken, quick to violence and adventurous, draws much of its inspiration from the Western.

As American colonists and immigrants spread westward fulfilling America's Manifest Destiny, tens of thousands of people took chances with their lives that most of us today would not dream of taking. They ventured into a largely unknown land, with the risk of arduous travel, the dangers of lawlessness and the hostility of the indigenous peoples. They left behind health care and consumer goods, families and social networks. It took people who were rugged and hard, courageous and fair to first settle, then tame and finally civilize the American West. While unquestionably there were scoundrels and outlaws to be suppressed and brought to justice, when have there not been in the world? There were also heroes aplenty— bringing law, clearing land, building communities and winning the West.

The real West of the 19th century morphed into a genre of pulp fiction and movie formulas in the early 20th century. The West seemed to provide a backdrop that was not only spectacular in setting, but without moral ambiguity. In the Western, like the murder mystery, right and wrong stand in clear relief. It is not hard to know who the good guys are and who the bad guys are—even without the white hats. The personification of the Western hero for three generations was John Wayne.

Of all the Western heroes of fact or fiction, none could be a better representative than John Wayne—the Duke. Art and life commingled in his on-screen roles and his off-screen identity. In fact, the Duke himself once quipped: "I play John Wayne in pretty much every film I do, and I've done pretty well so far, haven't I?"

In both life and in art, Wayne stood 6'41/2" tall, with broad shoulders, a ready grin and a willingness to use his fists. He was the perfect actor to embody the Western genre, because he saw life in the same terms: "Some people tell me everything isn't black and white. But I say why the hell not?"

Born Marion Morrison in 1907, Duke grew up in southern California and went to USC on a football scholarship. Like many young students of his day out there, he picked up work as a grip and an extra on the studio lots of the booming film industry that was flowing to Hollywood. In the 1920s and 1930s he worked his way up in the studio system, becoming John Wayne along the way, and principally playing fellows in white hats in B Westerns for studios like Republic and Universal. John Ford gave Wayne his breakout role as the Ringo Kid in *Stagecoach* in 1939.

Over four decades until his death in 1979, John Wayne came to be regarded the quintessential persona of the Western hero: direct, honest, reverent and something of a loner. His filmography as an actor includes 172 films and he holds the record for the actor with the most leading parts—142. Among the most famous of his pictures is the John Ford trilogy, *Fort Apache* (1948), *She Wore a Yellow Ribbon* (1949) and *Rio Grande* (1950). They teamed up again in 1956 for *The Searchers*. It was as Rooster Cogburn in *True Grit*, however, that Wayne earned his Academy Award as Best Actor in 1969.

Of course, John Wayne appeared in many non-Western starring roles as well, most commonly as a warrior—from *Back to Bataan*,(1945) *They Were Expendable* (1945) and *Sands of Iwo Jima* (1949) to *The Green Berets* (1968) two wars later. Even in his non-military roles, in movies like *Hatari* (1962), *Donovan's Reef* (1963) and *Hellfighters* (1968), Wayne always played the cowboy—with a bit of a swagger and devil-take-the-hindmost flare. "Courage is being scared to death," he said, "but saddling up anyway."

That swagger was subdued somewhat in *The Quiet Man* (1952), one of Wayne's least characteristic roles in many ways (but one of my favorites). Wayne plays Sean Thornton, an American heavy-weight fighter who has killed a man in the ring. Broken and humbled, Thornton returns to his ancestral home in rural Ireland to find peace and begin his life anew as a farmer—the quiet man. As it happens, Maureen O'Hara was there to see that he got more than he bargained for. The old cowboy in him surfaces at last, however, and the film comes to its rollicking climax in the most glorious and good-natured fist-fight sequence I can recall on screen. The whole village populace of Irish characters and cutups follows Sean and the Squire as they duke it out across town and countryside. The populace respectfully remains outside while the combatants pause to refresh themselves with a pint of Guinness and a bit of amiable chat before continuing the fight. The story could have been set . . . in Laredo.

It is true; we live in a more passive world than John Wayne did. For better or worse, as a real-life model, John Wayne is probably a hero whose day has passed. But we love him anyway. He took great pride in always wearing the white hat, and in being an outspoken patriot at a time when that itself was controversial. In all Wayne's characters there was an innate sense of decency that has always been a part of America's national character. Wayne shared that quality in real life as well: "I don't want ever to appear in a film that would embarrass a viewer. A man can take his wife, mother, and his daughter to one of my movies and never be ashamed or embarrassed for going."

CHAPTER 38

Bob Hope: Hero of Laughs

There is more than one way to prove a hero in time of war—without being a combatant. Chaplains and medics, doctors and nurses all serve close to the lines where war strips away the pretenses and the masks and makes dead men and goats and heroes.

Life as a combat soldier or sailor is intrinsically fearsome, dangerous and stressful. It's also often boring and demoralizing. The USO (United Services Organization) troupes that follow our servicemen and women around the globe provide a variety of services to men and women in uniform, perhaps known more well-known and appreciated than the entertainment they bring to military bases and troop deployments even in harm's way. Boosting the morale of men and women a long way from home, however admirable, of course, hardly seems to rank up there as a heroic occupation compared to the exigencies and dangers of military life. But then there was Bob Hope.

He was born Leslie Townes Hope in Eltham, England in May 1903, his English father was a stonemason and his

Welsh mother an aspiring concert singer. In 1907, Leslie's father brought the family to Cleveland, Ohio. Bob later quipped, "I left England at the age of four when I found out I couldn't be king."

After high school, Bob took dancing lessons, worked briefly as a newspaper reporter and tried amateur boxing under the name of Packy East. From the time he was 18, Bob teamed up with several partners in vaudeville song-and-dance acts. He spent most of his 20s on the vaudeville circuit, finally making it to New York. By then he was a solo act, and in 1933 got his first big Broadway break in a popular musical, *Roberta*. Over the next few years, Bob played in the *Ziegfield Follies of 1936* and *Red, Hot and Blue* with Ethel Merman and Jimmy Durante.

In May 1937, Bob signed his first radio contract with NBC. Over the years, Bob's show featured regulars including Jerry Colonna, the vocal group Six Hits and a Miss, Judy Garland, Frances Langford, Doris Day and Les Brown and His Band of Renown. Bob did his last regular radio show in April 1956.

Later that year, taking his radio show in the road, Hope traveled to Hollywood to make *The Big Broadcast of 1938*, his first major feature film. The "Road Pictures" with Bing Crosby and Dorothy Lamour made Hope a box office star. He went on to star in more than 50 feature films and earned the status of #1 at the box office. In the process, he introduced two Academy Award-winning songs: "Thanks for the Memory" in *The Big Broadcast of 1938* (which went on to become his signature song), and "Buttons and Bows" in *The Paleface* (1948). Another Hope classic was "Silver Bells" from *The Lemon Drop Kid*.

Though he was skeptical that the medium would survive, Bob made his debut on NBC television Easter Sunday, 1950. His first guest stars were Douglas Fairbanks, Jr., Dinah Shore and Beatrice Lillie. Over the next 46 years, he went on to do almost 300 television specials.

Movies and music, stand-up comedy, radio and television: Bob Hope was the consummate entertainer. His heroic mark in history, though, came performing for servicemen and women in the hot spots of the world.

For almost 60 years, at war or at peace, Bob traveled the globe to entertain the troops. Throughout World War II, Bob's radio shows were performed and aired from military bases and installations throughout the US and theaters of war in Europe and the South Pacific. His first trip into the combat area was in 1943 when he led a USO troupe to military bases in Britain, Africa, Sicily and Ireland. The next year his itinerary included the South Pacific. When Bob was asked to entertain the troops in Berlin supporting the Berlin Airlift in 1948, he began a Christmas custom that would last almost half a century. Every Christmas would see Bob and a band of Hollywood friends wherever the troops were around the globe.

With the end of the Vietnam conflict, Hope announced that his 1972 trip was his last Christmas show. Every Christmas that followed, however, Bob was somewhere doing shows at veterans' hospitals and military bases. In 1983, he went to Beirut. In 1987, the Christmas tour included stops across the Pacific, Atlantic and Indian Oceans and in the Persian Gulf. He did a goodwill tour in May 1990 to bases in England, Russia and Germany, and that Christmas entertained the troops of Operation Desert Storm in Saudi Arabia.

Bob was a pool hustler and an avid boxing and football fan, but golf was his passion. He played on over 2,000 courses around the globe—with golf's greatest pros and two generations of celebrities and presidents ("Golf is my profession. I tell jokes to pay my green fees"). The Bob Hope Desert Classic, the annual charity pro-am tournament he developed and hosted for years in Palm Springs has raised tens of millions for the Eisenhower Medical Center and 70 other deserving desert charities.

Bob was befriended by every President from Roosevelt to Clinton. His golfing buddies included Eisenhower, Nixon, Reagan, Bush and Clinton. In 1998, Queen Elizabeth II conferred on Bob an honorary knighthood— Knight Commander of the Most Excellent Order of the British Empire (KBE) in recognition of his contributions to entertainment and to his entertainment of the troops for almost 60 years.

The Guinness Book of Records cites Bob as the most honored entertainer in the world as both a professional and as a humanitarian. Though he never won an Oscar for his acting ("Oscar night at my house is called Passover"), the Academy of Motion Pictures Arts and Sciences honored him five times, with two honorary Oscars, two special awards and the Jean Hersholt Humanitarian Award.

Five times Bob was honored by Congress. In October 1997, Bob received one of his greatest tributes. Resolution 75 was unanimously passed by both houses making him an Honorary Veteran—the first individual so honored in United States history. He was feted in the U.S. Capitol Rotunda by members of congress, military personnel and veterans.

Among decades of honors, Bob's favorites were the 54 honorary doctorates he received from colleges and universities all across the land—St. Anselms to San Diego, Florida Southern to Gonzaga—Brown, Columbia, Pepperdine and Southern Methodist. He relished and took seriously the role of commencement speaker, often quipping: "My favorite subject was ancient history. Of course, when I went to school there wasn't much of it."

A whole generation of adults now exists who have never seen a Bob Hope movie.

CHAPTER 39

Jimmy Buffett: The Modern Mythic Hero

"Fruitcakes in the oven, fruitcakes on the bus,
There's a little bit of fruitcake left in every one of us"

Those archetypal classical heroes and big-stage heroes we need—Odysseus, Winston Churchill, King Arthur and the like. Of course, it is good for us individually and socially to have the great heroic virtues embodied in larger than life historic figures for us to emulate and from whom we draw inspiration for ourselves and for humanity.

We also need prophets and sages to remind us not to take ourselves too seriously—folk heroes of our own time and place to refresh us and remind us that the Emperor often parades naked in the street. Will Rogers was such a figure in his generation and Mark Twain for a generation before that.

In medieval times, royal and noble households often included a jester who organized the entertainment both public and private. Such was the privileged position of the jester, oft thought a fool, that he could exercise his sagacity cloaked in wit to his patron and surrounding courtiers. Like Rogers and Twain, the quintessential jester could make his audience laugh and celebrate life and communicate serious truths about human life at the same time.

It was a historic early September night in Boston, and in the storied confines of hallowed Fenway Park. But the Red Sox were on the road. I emerged from Kenmore Square Station into a sea of tropical pastels and hot primary colors. Beachcomber hats, grass skirts, parrots and pirates—and beer. From their 20s to their 70s, the crowd streaming toward the gates of Fenway were there to greet their hero—with no less joy and adulation than greeted Wellington in London upon his return from Waterloo. Jimmy Buffett was in town.

For only the second time in its history, Fenway Park became a concert venue that weekend for Jimmy Buffett and the Coral Reefer Band. Parrotheads from Maine to Maryland gathered, 40,000 at a time, for two weekend concerts with Jimmy. They came to party, to connect and to sing along with Jimmy in a celebration of life.

Go to a Beach Boys concert and it's a trip—right back into the 1960s. Energetic but late middle-aged men singing the songs they wrote and popularized 40 years ago as teens, "In My Room" and "Be True To Your School" and tapping into recognition in its late middle-aged audience, who pretend for the evening that they are young again. The experience is pure nostalgia.

It's a different dynamic entirely at Fenway Park. The experience is now. Extra beer vending stations are set up in the concourse. The crowd filing in is already pretty mellow. But there's never a cross word or a faded smile. Beach balls by the score bounce over the crowd for three solid hours. By the third number the sweet smell of pot wafts over the grandstands. Worse still, people are openly smoking cigarettes and nobody seems to care.

A wall of upbeat sound envelopes the stadium. With the exception of one or two new covers for the season's tour, Jimmy doesn't so much sing *to* his jazzed-up fans as lead a mammoth sing-along—40,000 people, who all know the words, waving their arms and bellowing out "Fins to the left; fins to right." Jimmy's no need to invite the crowd to "All please rise for the national anthem." No one is sitting down anyway. The anthem, of course, is "Margaritaville," and they know all three stanzas. And a deliriously happy time is had by all.

It's one of those things that either you get or you don't, as Parrotheads will tell you. A singer is just a singer (no matter how ardent their fans), but Jimmy Buffett is a hero—to several millions of people. The only parallel in the recent history of pop culture and music is perhaps the Grateful Dead. The medium is the same, though the message and its followers are different. Still, Deadheads understand.

For more than 30 years, Jimmy Buffett wrote and performed a canon of songs across every genre of popular music. Country, folk, rock, ballads, blues and gospel all find expression in Buffett's music. Beyond the music, however, is a consistent philosophy of life that has matured and aged with time, as Buffett and his audience have added the years together. Early Buffett classics like "Grapefruit Juicy Fruit" and "Rag Top Day" still have a place in the hearts of Parrotheads, but they are not what Jimmy was writing and singing as a man in his late 50s. His lyrics and his repertoire express the experiences of life—parenting, pacing the cage, doubting, confirming, evaluating experience. "Come Monday" has seen enough of life to become "The Coast of Carolina."

Both the music and lyrics of Buffett's songline are upbeat, life-affirming and positive. If those legendary Jimmy Buffett concerts were pure escapism, the message they delivered is at once light-hearted and serious. The gospel according to Buffett reminds us that it is a good thing to have play and enjoy life—fun tickets are good. Virtues like tolerance, compassion, friendliness and lack-of-uptightness are a cultivated state of mind. Like the little boy in the "Emperor's New Clothes," Jimmy Buffett mocked the inanities and hypocrisies of government, business, church and sundry social conventions that his Parrothead crowd recognizes as a nakedness in contemporary society.

Buffett's is a libertarian gospel—live and let live. At the same time, there is a strong social conscience in his message. Care of the earth and our ecosystems is important. Giving back is more important than climbing the career ladder. Parrotheads embrace the classic *carpe diem* theme and seize the day, but they also party with a purpose. In fact, that's the motto of the over 200 Parrothead clubs across the country. Each year the clubs raise millions for conservation causes, medical research and local charities.

As a man, Jimmy Buffett was a successful and level-headed businessman—in addition to being a superb musician and entertainer. After all, you don't stay permanently in Margaritaville and *live* 40 years, let alone build a vertically integrated music, entertainment, hospitality and retailing empire.

It was all built on a myth. The inside joke between Jimmy Buffett and the Parrotheads who "get it" is that everyone knows it. You might as well party like there's no tomorrow, because there might well not be. At the same time, as Jimmy avers lyrically, now he gets up about the time he used to go to bed. Margaritaville is a sweet place to hang around for a while, but you can't stay there any more than you can stay in Toyland or Never Never Land. Like the canons of the finest poets, the themes of his lyrics matured, but his music lost none of its spark and creative energy.

Among the consistent themes of Buffett's lyrics over the years was the search for heroes. His songs are full of the quest of Ulysses and the adventure of Captain Cook, both in their water and island setting and in their search for experience. "The Captain and the Kid," "He Went to Paris," "One Particular Harbor," "Last Mango in Paris," A Pirate Looks at Forty," and many other Buffett classics portray the questing hero. Jimmy Buffett became a hero himself to his fan base promoting heroism and articulating the universal theme of the quester. Thank you, Jolly Man.

CHAPTER 40

The Hero with a Thousand Faces

We have come a long way from the questing hero of Odysseus to the questing hero of Jimmy Buffett.

We didn't talk about Adam Smith, whose monumental book *The Wealth of Nations* laid the foundations of the mercantile economy. We didn't mention Dwight Eisenhower. Yup, he was the Supreme Allied Commander in Europe during WWII, but his visionary creation of the Interstate Highway system changed the country more than any other single political accomplishment in the second half of the 20th century. And after more than 40 years at the helm of Duke University basketball, even for hard-core college basketball fans, it is difficult to keep track of the awards and honors that Coach Mike Krzyzewski garnered over the years.

We didn't speak of Martin Luther King, St. Thomas More, St. Augustine, Isambard Kingdom Brunel, Frederick Douglas or Martin Luther. Absent also are Golda Meir, Jackie Robinson, John F. Kennedy, William Wilberforce, Christa McAuliffe, Elvis, St. Paul and John Glenn. Margaret

Thatcher, Louis Armstrong, and Indira Gandhi. Cal Ripkin, Lou Gehrig, Margaret Chase Smith, Arthur Ashe, Gordie Howe and Vince Lombardi, George M. Cohan and Irving Berlin; the Duke of Wellington, George Frederick Handel and the Four Chaplains. Richard Arkwright, Flora MacDonald, Thomas Edison and Jonas Salk. John Cabot, Francis of Assisi and Mother Elizabeth Seton. And, yes, I really skipped those heroes of our Independence and the Civil War generals. They get a lot of attention, and I wouldn't know where to end.

Any of these names and many more might be on your own list—heroes of sport, culture, moral vision, political leadership, bravery and faith. You can look it up.

Regardless of how or how much I admire the individuals, from King Arthur and Robin Hood to Stan Rogers and Mary Somerville, mentioned or championed in these pages, however, everyone has to build their own pantheon of heroes. There is no such thing as a politically correct list. Our heroes reflect what we are, not what we think we are supposed to be. As in so many other areas of life, of course, we can fake it for public consumption. Plenty of people do. We praise loudly those already receiving the applause of the crowd; that is easy and makes us one of the crowd. In reality, though, we secretly know the world is full of popular bums.

Where we find heroes depends upon where we look.

The Heroism of the Stooges

Heroes come in all shapes and sizes, as we have seen. Heroism doesn't demand a gender or body type; a tiny figure like Mother Theresa or Harriet Tubman can be as heroic as an athlete like Michael Jordan or a towering powerhouse like John Wayne.

I would be hardly the first to suggest that the kinds of heroes that exist today for children are pretty vapid. Our schools and children's books, public library programs and television are all providing our children and grandchildren with value messages quite different from those reflected in the stories of *my* heroes. Speaking of popular bums . . . compared to contemporary video games and cartoons, the Three Stooges were a fount of life lessons.

Three generations of mothers are now cringing, but it is true. The Three Stooges are more culturally edifying and infinitely more imaginative than most of what now entertains boys on television these days. Yes, it's a guy thing. Just three dumb schmucks, Moe, Larry and Curly, who tackled the world head on, with optimism, enthusiasm and *joi d'vivre*. They ventured into the wide world ignorantly but fearlessly, flinched from no one's pedigree or social status, bore no self-consciousness or insecurity.

Episode after episode, the loveable mugs waded into life. The Stooges were laughable as lawyers, bungled as butlers, made a hash of haberdashery. They were bums and bankers, empty-minded professors and plasterers, cabbies and mad scientists. They were hustlers, conmen and victims. Pretty generally the idea was that they were just trying to get ahead. To better their lives. One way or another, they always meant well.

Behind all the mayhem and comic-strip violence, the Three Stooges reinforced in us some valuable lessons: no matter how many knocks you take, you play through the pain. You stick with your pals. No matter how many times things don't work out like you planned, you dust yourself off and start over again. No matter how many times life rebuffs you and how many failures you've had, there is always something else to try.

Winston Churchill dignified the Stooges' message summarily: "Success is going from failure to failure with no loss of enthusiasm."

After All, Heroes aren't Perfect

Alas, yes, heroes, like everyone else, have their frailties and their limitations. Not since the days of the myth-making Romans and Greeks have heroes been gods or demigods. Whatever the Noble Qualities that are displayed by an individual in heroic stance or actions, they are people. All right. So the Three Stooges aren't exactly perfect role models. Which of our heroes is?

Admiring the heroism of great and noble men and women does not mean they necessarily led completely admirable lives, nor that we would want our children to emulate their lives. The world would little appreciate a whole gaggle of John Wayne wannabees running around. We can thoroughly admire Winston Churchill and his incomparable role in history without wanting to smoke his cigars.

In our heroes, instead, we find the highest aspirations of human experience. They prompt us not to imitate their lives, but to seek the best in our own. Preachers, teachers, psychics and mothers rarely hesitate to give us *their* opinions. At the end of the day, however, we are the only ones who define that "best" for ourselves.

There is a danger, on the other hand, to requiring too much of our heroes. The closer we demand our heroes share all of our own virtues and values the closer we come to making very complacent heroes of ourselves in our own eyes. That's narcissism.

George Bernard Shaw famously observed in *Maxims for Revolutionists*: "The reasonable man adapts himself to the world: the unreasonable one persists in trying to adapt the world to himself. Therefore all progress depends on the unreasonable man." In a sense, all heroes are unreasonable people. They are motivated to their heroic stance by something other than reason. Often, their heroic actions are not those that most of us would describe as reasonable or the rational thing to do. It just isn't rational to risk your life, or reasonable to expend it in service to others.

After all, as the Old Bean remarked, "If we're all on this earth to help others, what are the others here for?"

Finding Those Heroes

If where we find heroes depends upon where we look, of course, it bears remembering that other people are looking at us. At you and me. This is the time in the program when the conventional thing to write is that we are all heroes or potential heroes in the eyes of those around us—our children, extended family, neighbors, bingo buddies and co-workers, church family, garden club or lodge brothers. Our lives are more closely scrutinized by those around us than we routinely acknowledge to ourselves. We know that from how we evaluate the lives of others.

It is true of course that heroes have always lived amongst us unawares. And, yes, heroes, like saints, dwell quietly in our midst: teachers, caregivers, rec league coaches, nurses and Salvation Army workers, firefighters and youth group leaders, all those who give texture to our society, touch our lives and give of themselves to do it.

Maybe it is Stan Rogers, the hero-gone-too-soon, who provides us with the greatest lessons. First, that since we know not how short our lives might be, anything we wish to accomplish with that life we'd better be about. Second, that the work gone-too-soon heroes might have left the world—the music, the ideas, the ministry to human need—remains to be done.

"What we are to be, we are now becoming." Yes, it is true of people, you and me, and everyone who is touched and influenced by our lives, and it is true of nations and societies.

On the individual level, we can be much defined by those who are our heroes. As an American society (or as a New England society, or a Spokane society, or a Winslow, Arizona society), we are defined by those who are our corporate heroes. One can only hope they are not the same as those the media finds necessarily *newsworthy*.

This book of heroes is complete. Our personal book of heroes, though, is never finished. It is edited, amended, added to and appended as we continue to become, as we continue to grow. As our book grows and changes, so too does the kind of hero we are in the eyes of others, and the kind of goat or hero we might prove to be if called upon by circumstances we cannot yet imagine.

We do not pick our heroes in a vacuum. They come from what we *prize* as nobility. They come from what we value in people and in ourselves. They come from our collective experience as a culture, a sub-culture, a nation, a state, a community and a family.

Who will be our Great American heroes of the 21st century?

What footprints will we leave on the sands of time?

Whose hero will *we* be?

www.ingramcontent.com/pod-product-compliance
Lightning Source LLC
Chambersburg PA
CBHW021622120626
46545CB00001B/347

9 781956 452709